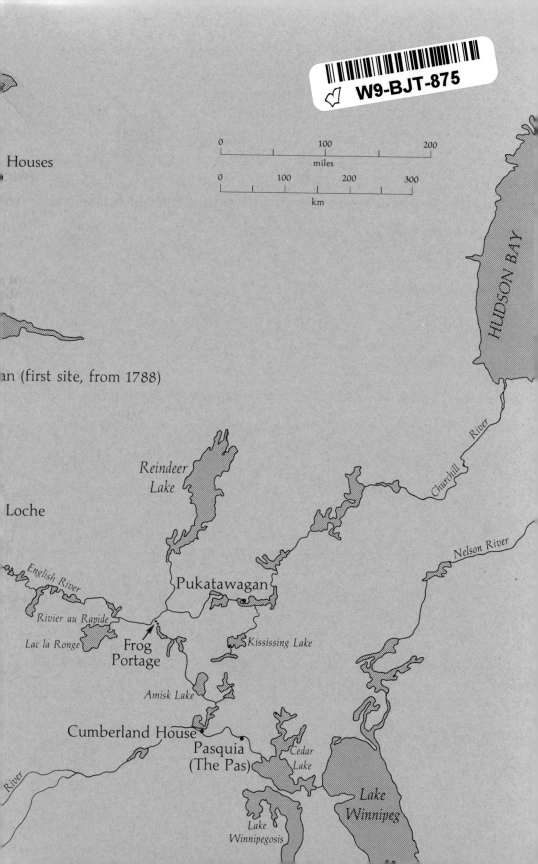

Houses

an (first site, from 1788)

Loche

HUDSON BAY

Churchill River

Reindeer Lake

Nelson River

English River

Pukatawagan

Rivier au Rapide

Lac la Ronge

Frog Portage

Kississing Lake

Amisk Lake

Cumberland House

Pasquia (The Pas)

Cedar Lake

River

Lake Winnipegosis

Lake Winnipeg

0		100		200

miles

0		100		200		300

km

THE

ENGLISH

RIVER

BOOK

Rupert's Land Record
Society Series
Jennifer S.H. Brown, Editor

1 The English River Book
A North West Company Journal
and Account Book of 1786
Harry W. Duckworth

THE
ENGLISH
RIVER
BOOK

A North West Company Journal
and Account Book of 1786

Edited with an Introduction
by Harry W. Duckworth

McGill-Queen's University Press
Montreal and Kingston, London, Buffalo

© McGill-Queen's University Press 1990
ISBN 0-7735-0714-0
Legal deposit 1st quarter 1990
Bibliothèque nationale du Québec

∞

Printed in Canada on acid-free paper

This book has been published with the help of a grant
from the Social Science Federation of Canada, using funds
provided by the Social Sciences and Humanities Research
Council of Canada.

Canadian Cataloguing in Publication Data

Main entry under title:
The English river book
Includes index.
ISBN 0-7735-0714-0
1. North West Company – History – Sources. 2. Fur
trade – Canada – History – 18th century – Sources.
3. Northwest, Canadian – History – To 1870 – Sources.
4. North West Company – History. 5. Fur trade –
Canada – History – 18th century. 6. Northwest,
Canadian – History – To 1870. I. Duckworth, Harry W.
FC3212.3.E64 1989   971.2'01   C89-090183-X
F1060.E64 1989

Endpapers: The English River district
and its approaches in the 1780s

To Mary Lynn

CONTENTS

TABLES

MAPS

PREFACE

The document published here, the "English River Book" of 1786, invites the interest of historians of the fur trade and the northwest part of Canada for a number of reasons. As North West Company documents go, it is early, apparently the earliest of its kind to survive. The Journal contained in it, though brief, is our only strictly contemporary record from Peter Pond's original Athabasca Fort at the period when the fur trade in that region was just starting to open up the country. Some twenty-one Indians are named in this Journal, the earliest Indian names on record for Athabasca, and the careers of several of them may be traced in later documents (appendix A). The Account Book provides a complete list of the men in the North West Company's establishments at Athabasca and on the Churchill (the "English River" of the traders), and further research into the histories of these men (appendix B) has shown the extent to which some of them formed an élite force of *commis*, interpreters, and canoemen as the northwest trade expanded. The brief Cree vocabulary and the inventories of trade goods, although dry reading, are authentic early documents which deserve the attention of specialists.

I first became aware of the English River Book about nine years ago, while browsing through the collection of North West Company papers in the Hudson's Bay Company Archives in Winnipeg. Eventually I realized that few scholars had ever heard of it. The document presumably came to the Hudson's Bay Company in 1821, along with other papers relating to the North West Company servants who were being taken over at the amalgamation, but its survival can only have been an accident, since the accounts it contains were thirty-five years old in 1821, and only a handful of the individuals mentioned in the book were still active in the fur trade. This haphazard survival of course is typical of North West Company records, many of which owe their present existence to the collecting energies of Roderick McKenzie and Senator Louis-François R. Masson, to Lord Selkirk's high-handed seizures, or to other lucky chances.

I wish to thank the Secretary, Hudson's Bay Company, for permission to publish the English River Book in its entirety. This document, which is classified as F.2/1, is from the holdings of the Hudson's Bay Company Archives, Provincial Archives of Manitoba. I also record my thanks to Professor Jennifer Brown, General Editor of the Rupert's Land Record Society, for her encouragement and advice, particularly in arranging for publication. Dr Mary Black-Rogers read an early version of the manuscript and shared with me her unrivalled knowledge of the Athabasca and English River voyageurs of the early nineteenth century. Dr C. Stuart Houston provided a full review of the manuscript and made a number of incisive suggestions, most of which I have incorporated into the text, Dr Richard Virr of the McGill University Libraries and Special Collections located a number of North West Company letters in those collections, which were useful in this and other research. It is a particular pleasure to thank Mrs Shirlee Anne Smith, Keeper of the Hudson's Bay Company Archives, and her staff, for their patient help over some twelve years of research in that splendid collection.

Harry W. Duckworth
Winnipeg, 31 January 1989

INTRODUCTION

THE ENGLISH RIVER BOOK

Hudson's Bay Company Archives document HBCA F.2/1 is a parchment-bound book containing seventy-three foolscap pages. The outside cover is labelled "1786/English River/Book/R.R.R."[1] The document is part of the archives' collection of North West Company papers. Its principal contents are the accounts of the North West Company's employees at English River (the North Westers' name for the Churchill River) for the trading season of 1785–6. The men whose accounts appear were employed at the familiar English River posts at Île-à-la-Crosse and Lac La Ronge and in the Rat River country, but also at Athabasca, which had not yet been made a separate district.[2] Apart from individual accounts for ninety-seven men listing their wages, incidental earnings, and charges against them, the English River Book also contains several lists of remnant trading goods from the end of the season, a short Cree vocabulary of words for trading goods, and other bookkeeping details. In addition, the first item, which occupies seventeen pages, is a daily Journal. This Journal was kept at the first Athabasca trading post, Peter Pond's "Old Establishment" on the lower Athabasca River, which was to be replaced in 1788 by Fort Chipewyan. The Journal begins on 1 April, 1786, with the start of the spring trade, and continues at the post until 9 May, when the journalist left on the outward canoe voyage to Lac La Pluie. He continued to keep the Journal as he went until 31 May, the day before the brigade was to arrive at Île-à-la-Crosse. This Journal provides a uniquely early glimpse of Athabasca under the pioneering direction of Peter Pond.

This Journal is apparently the earliest North West Company post journal in existence. Later journals from the same Company are scattered but fairly plentiful, and examples from Athabasca and its dependencies have survived in reasonable numbers from the first decade of the 1800s. The only other North West Company survivor from the 1780s is a special case, the journal kept by Edward Umfreville in the summer of 1784, when he was exploring an alternative route from Lake Nipigon to the Winnipeg River for the company. This interesting document was published long ago,[3] but it is not concerned with trade.

Present knowledge of the opening up of Athabasca, the richest province of the North West Company's domain, is derived almost entirely from the writings of Alexander Mackenzie and his cousin Roderick, and before 1787 all their information was obtained at second hand. The 1786 Journal in the English River Book, however, is strictly contemporary. It was written at the Athabasca post itself, and it provides many vivid details which enrich our understanding of how the fur trade was established in that region.

HBCA F.2/1 appears largely to have escaped the attention of fur trade historians. A typewritten note by A.S. Morton, now attached inside the front cover of the document, shows that he had studied it in 1933 and identified the journalist, but his great *History of the Canadian West* (Morton, 1973) shows no sign of this research. The Hudson's Bay Company Archives has a transcript of F.2/1 which, according to the catalogue of copies, was prepared for Mr R.H. Fleming a few years later, but no result of his studies seems to have been published.[4] It is therefore felt that the publication of the English River Book in its entirety will be of value to historians of the early northwest fur trade.

Although the Journal is not signed, its author is almost certainly identified by the entry of 1 April, in which the journalist wrote, "Derry Should go this Summer and build a fort at the lack des Esclave and that I would go there next fall with the goods." Cuthbert Grant, later a North West Company partner and father of the Métis leader of the same name, is known to have taken a brigade to Great Slave Lake for the North West Company in the fall of 1786, and, as A.S. Morton said in the note already mentioned above, this correlation seems to show that the Journal was kept by Cuthbert Grant. All of the clerks and *commis* listed in the accounts in the English Book can be eliminated in one way or another. Charles Boyer, Alexis

Derry, and Peter Pond himself are mentioned in the third person in the Journal. Jurial Baldwin is known to have spent the winter of 1785–6 in Rat River (see his biography, page 136). Notes to the inventories show that both Tourangeau and Toussaint Lesieur remained in English River for the summer of 1786. The Account Book, however, which is in the same hand as the Journal, contains entries for Baldwin's men on 13 June, showing that the journalist did not remain in the district but probably went on to Lac La Pluie with the book itself. That Cuthbert Grant was present in the English River district in 1785–6 is shown by an entry in the account of Joseph Preux, a *devant* in the Athabasca brigade, "To Mr Cuthbert Grant for a Gun." As is noted below (page xix), there is some evidence that Grant built and occupied a trading fort on the north shore of Lake Athabasca during part of the trading season of 1785–6, and the date of commencement of the Journal, 1 April 1786, may be when he returned to the main establishment.

PETER POND AND ATHABASCA

The northwest trade which was re-established with English capital after the Conquest of Canada at first simply reproduced the pre-Conquest trade established by La Vérendrye and his successors. Indeed, it is reasonable to suspect, though we cannot prove, that the post-Conquest trade was rebuilt by the brains as well as the shoulders of the veterans of New France. Taking trade goods to the Churchill River, the route to the far northwest, was however a new achievement for which credit is consistently given to the Yorkshiremen, Joseph and Thomas Frobisher. With their brother Benjamin and his network of investment partners to support them, the Frobishers had achieved a strong and dependable position in the northwest trade by the early 1770s[5].

In the winter of 1773–4, Joseph Frobisher and a sometime Hudson's Bay Company servant, Louis Primot, operated a trading post on the present Namew Lake, just north of the main course of the Saskatchewan River and one lake removed from Cumberland or Pine Island Lake where Samuel Hearne the next summer founded Cumberland House. At the northeast end of Namew Lake the Sturgeon-Weir River falls in, a rapid-filled stream which, followed to its source, permits canoes to come within a few hundred yards of the Churchill River. In the spring of 1774, as soon as the ice had broken up, Frobisher and his men proceeded up the Sturgeon-Weir River to Frog Portage, the link with the Churchill, and there they intercepted and traded with the Athabasca Indians as they made their usual trading voyage to Churchill Fort, the Hudson's Bay Company's establishment on Hudson Bay.

The success of this trading episode was immense. While Frobisher left for Grand Portage with his furs, Primot remained to build a permanent post on the Churchill River itself. The next season Joseph and Thomas Frobisher, with six canoes, wintered at Frog Portage. Although this location was ideal for intercepting the spring convoys of Indians heading for Churchill Fort, it proved impossible to get adequate food there during the winter. Next summer, the Hudson's Bay Company people at Cumberland House learned that one or two of the Frobishers' men had starved to death during the winter, and that another had been shot by an Indian for cannibalism; five more men were sent overland in December to be supported by the traders on the Saskatchewan. In 1775–6 the Frobishers, now joined by the celebrated trader, Alexander Henry the elder, made their winter quarters on Beaver (now Amisk) Lake, partway up the Sturgeon-Weir River, where provisions were more dependable. In the spring their trade with the Indians going down to Churchill was again a spectacular success, and flushed with the confidence of their superior numbers they firmly suppressed the attempts of Robert Longmoor, a Hudson's Bay Company servant, who had been sent up from Cumberland House to recapture part of the trade.[6]

But where were these furs coming from, and how much greater would the profits be if the traders could penetrate further to the northwest? The Frobishers had sent Primot with two canoes to establish a settlement farther up Churchill River in the summer of 1775, but Primot did not go very far (it is presumed that he stopped at the present Primeau Lake), and again was short of provisions.[7] Accordingly, Thomas Frobisher himself proceeded up the Churchill with four canoes in the summer of 1776 and established a fort at Île-à-la-Crosse.[8] Living in winter was assured at this post – Île-à-la-Crosse was to become famous for its whitefish – but Frobisher himself actually wintered on the Saskatchewan, and Louis Primot was left in charge at the new settlement. In the spring of 1777, Frobisher went up the Sturgeon-Weir River to the Churchill as soon as the ice permitted, met Primot with the Indians coming down, and concluded another successful trade. Both Thomas Frobisher and Primot returned with the furs to Montreal.[9]

The expansion of the fur trade to the north faltered somewhat in 1777–8, and Île-à-la-Crosse itself was apparently abandoned. Beaver Lake was occupied by new traders, Tute and Saint-Germain, who were perhaps in the Frobishers' employ.[10] Meanwhile, the number of traders on the Saskatchewan had increased to the point that the amount of goods available to buy furs far outweighed the supply. Alexander Mackenzie tells us that some of these traders put their surplus goods into a joint stock which they entrusted to Peter Pond, one of their number, who was to try to penetrate to the fabled Athabasca country itself.[11] Pond passed Cumberland House with five canoes on 26 May 1778, heading north.[12]

One year later, starving and with only three canoes remaining after accidents on the return trip, he reappeared with the news that he had traded 140 packs of furs, mainly parchment and coat beaver, but had been forced to leave most of them behind for want of canoes to bring them out.[13] Pond had discovered a new region, cold, remote, and rich in furs. Through the inattention of the Frobishers, whose most experienced man, Primot, had been in Montreal in 1777–8, the traders who had opened up the Churchill River to trade can have had only a small share in the success of Pond's adventure. As long as he remained in the northwest trade, Peter Pond regarded himself as the proprietor of Athabasca, and the hardships he had endured and the enterprise he had displayed gave him strong claim to that title; but almost at once it began to slip from his hands. Pond arrived at Grand Portage, in the summer of 1779, to find that the northwest traders had formed a consortium to exploit the fur grounds more effectively since the state of war in Canada had permitted them to bring up only limited trade goods from Montreal. This consortium sent thirteen canoes to the Churchill River, commanded not by Pond but by Jean-Étienne Waddens, another trader.[14] The bulk of the Athabasca furs, which Pond had cached there, were retrieved and must have formed a large part of the 200 packs that Waddens brought out in the spring of 1780.[15]

Although it has generally been assumed that Peter Pond returned to Athabasca in 1779 to help retrieve the furs, there is no real evidence that he did so, and he was not in the northwest in 1780–1. In 1781–2 he was at Lac La Ronge in the Churchill River basin, alongside Waddens and nominally cooperating with him. The two did not get along – the difference may have stemmed from 1779, when Waddens had been put in charge of the second expedition to Athabasca – and in March 1782 Waddens died of a gunshot wound, suffered under mysterious circumstances in the presence of Pond and his clerk, Toussaint Lesieur.[16] With Waddens gone, the rapidly expanding fur country of the Churchill and Athabasca, known collectively as the English River district, was placed under the command of Pond and Patrick Small, an associate or protégé of Simon McTavish, who was now emerging into the leadership of the northwest trade. Pond and Small took sixteen canoes into English River in the fall of 1782.[17] In this season, it was later said, the goods reached the upper Churchill so late that only a single canoe, lightly laden, could be got across Portage La Loche into the Athabasca country, and that party found that the natives had been decimated by smallpox. By the following season, however, the situation had improved, and henceforth it appears that a permanent settlement was maintained in Athabasca.[18]

In the summer of 1784, the winterers came to Grand Portage to learn that a new, sixteen-share North West Company had been hammered out in Montreal the previous winter, and that this was intended to have a monopoly in the northwest trade. The Frobishers and Simon McTavish were the major shareholders, and the Frobishers were to be "Directors" or agents at Montreal. Peter Pond was offered one share in this company, with which he was not satisfied, and, instead of taking an outfit back into Athabasca, he went down to Montreal.[19] The English River and Athabasca regions appear to have been placed in the hands of Patrick Small and Nicholas Montour in 1784–5.[20] Each of these men had been given two shares in the sixteen-share company,[21] and their assignment to English River shows the importance which the company attached to those regions.

Pond's first intention when he came down to Canada, according to Alexander Mackenzie, had been to form a new company in opposition to the North West Company, and he associated himself with Peter Pangman, a seasoned Saskatchewan River trader who had been completely excluded from the North West Company arrangements.[22] Pangman formerly had traded in partnership with John Ross, one of the shareholders in the "North West Company" of 1779, and in the fall of 1784 Ross and Pangman began arrangements to send a substantial outfit to the northwest in the following spring.[23] The supplier of goods to this "New Concern" was to be the Montreal firm of Gregory and McLeod, which had never been involved in the northwest trade before although it had shipped large quantities of goods to Detroit and Michilimackinac during the previous few years.

Peter Pond may have continued with Ross and Pangman for several months, but he had other matters on his mind. Foremost, it appears, was his concern simply to get recognition for his discovery of Athabasca, and for a theory that the Athabasca drainage basin could be reached by ascending a river from the Pacific. He presented the first of his famous maps to the American Congress on 1 March 1785, but apparently received no encouragement. Soon after he was back in Canada, where the widow of Jean-Étienne Waddens had succeeded in starting some kind of criminal proceedings against Pond and Lesieur for the murder of her husband.[24] As has often been stated, no evidence has been found that Pond was actually tried for Waddens' murder, and it seems possible that the Frobisher brothers, directors of the North West Company, used their influence to get him out of this trouble. Some surviving documents suggest that the Frobishers obtained an interview for Pond with Henry Hamilton, lieutenant governor of Quebec, at which Pond presented a copy of his map and explained his geographical conclusions. By now, Pond was evidently reconciled to the North West Company, and a petition to Hamilton dated 18 April 1785, asking for a monopoly of the northwest fur trade, was signed by him as a member of the company, though the Frobishers probably prepared the document.[25]

The monopoly was not granted, and when Peter Pond returned to Athabasca in the fall of 1785, in charge again of the North West Company's trade in that region, a strong opponent, the New Concern's John Ross, went there too.

Not much is know about John Ross. He first appears in 1777–8, when he was trading at Pasquia (The Pas) on the lower Saskatchewan.[26] The next reference is in the trade licences for 1779, when he was to take one canoe with nine men to Grand Portage under the sponsorship of Joseph Frobisher; he had one share in the sixteen-share company formed for 1779–80.[27] The following year he and Peter Pangman took four canoes to Grand Portage.[28] Ross's trade in 1780–1, at least, was on the Assiniboine River in southern Manitoba.[29] With the creation of the opposition to the North West

Company by Pangman and Ross in 1784, the New Concern backed by Gregory and McLeod, John Ross accepted the task of taking the rivalry into Athabasca. It would be here that the stakes would be highest, the victory most decisive.

The Trading Season of 1785–6

At noon on 3 September, 1785, Peter Pond landed at the Hudson's Bay Company post of Cumberland House, where he spoke briefly with William Walker, the summer master, and traded fresh meat from some Indians in return for an eight-gallon keg of rum. He had fourteen canoes with him.[30] During the next few weeks a further eight canoes passed Cumberland House for "the Northward," for on 20 September William Walker noted in his journal that "the total canoes for the forementioned quarter is 22."[31] An analysis of the manpower available to the North West Company in English River in 1785–6, as determined from the English River Book, suggests that the total canoes which that company sent into the district in 1785 was fourteen to sixteen, so that six or eight probably belonged to the New Concern. According to Roderick McKenzie, John Ross was in command at Athabasca, while Alexander Mackenzie, who had been recruited by the New Concern from among the employees of Gregory and McLeod, was in charge at English River itself. It is likely that Laurent Leroux, one of Ross and Pangman's clerks, accompanied Ross to Athabasca in 1785, as he did in 1786.[32] François Barille, who was contracted to "Pengmain & Ross" to go to "la Rivière des Anglais" on 27 December, 1784, or Clément Pera, hired for the same place on 13 May, 1785, may have been the guide who took Ross and Mackenzie up to Île-à-la-Crosse.[33]

Mackenzie stopped somewhere on the Churchill, probably at Île-à-la-Crosse itself, alongside Patrick Small, the North West Company master. John Ross, with perhaps four canoes and no more than two dozen men, crossed Portage La Loche and proceeded down the Clearwater River and the Athabasca. He would have found Pond's fort, strongly manned by three clerks and forty-six voyageurs, near the place where the Athabasca River enters its delta at Lake Athabasca.[34] The English River Book Journal makes no mention of a fort belonging to Ross or the New Concern. Instead, the single reference to Ross in the Journal (under 20 April, 1786) indicates that Ross had spent a least part of the winter somewhere beyond

Pond's establishment, for the English Chief, one of the most important trading Chipewyans, was suspected of waiting for Ross "below." Ross had told the Indians that he was trading for the Hudson's Bay Company, "and they Seem in General to believe it."[35] Such a claim would have had great force in the ears of these Indians, some of whom had been accustomed to taking their furs on the arduous journey to Churchill Fort, until Peter Pond had come among them.

One likely consequence of the existence of opposing interests at Athabasca would be the establishment of new outposts; such a strategy would be of special value to Pond, since it would allow him to exploit his numerical advantage. The Journal entry for 10 April which refers to "the old Chief that was with Derry," seems to suggest that Alexis Derry, one of Pond's clerks, had been at an outpost during the winter, although there is no indication of its whereabouts. Another outpost seems to had been established during this season by Pond's second-in-command, Cuthbert Grant. Pond's map of July 1787 shows a trading fort, No 20, on the north side of the Lake of the Hills, that is, Lake Athabasca; this fort must therefore have been established before the date of this map.[36] The site was noted as "Grant's House" by Peter Fidler, who passed it in August 1791; this must mean that it was built by Cuthbert Grant.[37] Since Grant was at Great Slave Lake in 1786–7, it is likely that he established the Lake Athabasca post in 1785–6, in response to competition from the New Concern. If Grant was absent from the main Athabasca fort during the winter, this may explain why the English River Book Journal does not commence until 1 April when he had returned.

The Journal shows that Pond was planning a large expansion for the next season. New posts were to be established at Lac des Esclaves (Great Slave Lake, by Alexis Derry) and at Rivière La Paix (Peace River, by Charles Boyer) in the summer, and the Journal gives the names of the men who were hired to winter there. The two canoe loads of "sundries," which were sent from Île-à-la-Crosse to meet the outward Athabasca brigade on the upper Churchill on 31 May, 1786 and forwarded to Pond in care of Alexis Derry, would probably have been intended to complete the assortment of goods for these summer expeditions.

Apart from competition, a second reason for expanding the trade is also suggested in the Journal. All the native peoples of the region, for some hundreds of miles around – Crees from the south, Beaver

Indians from Peace River, and Chipewyans from Great Slave Lake and beyond – were resorting to Pond's fort, and occasional fights that resulted were bound to discourage Pond's customers. The planned new post at Great Slave Lake was to be for the Chipewyans, and Pond instructed the Big Chief, one of their principal men, to go to that post in future. The Peace River post would be for the Beaver Indians; within a few years, as well, it had become the major source of provisions for the Athabasca trade.[38] Another outpost, dependent on Pond's fort, was soon established for the Crees on the Athabasca River, some distance above the main fort.[39]

The Journal throws us immediately into the middle of the spring trade. A Chipewyan band, about twenty men whose leader was called the Big Chief, had just arrived. It is important to remember that Pond's customers in 1786 were farflung, since his fort and that of Ross, his opponent, were the only trading posts north of Portage La Loche, and the trading Indians would have come hundreds of miles in some instances. The Big Chief was likely one of the principal trading Indians on the Mackenzie River and was mentioned frequently in journals of 1800–1 and 1806–7. Some twenty other individual Indians are named in the Journal of whom seven or eight seem to be recognizable in later fur trade documents (see appendix A). The Beaver Indian called the Tétons, described by Philip Turnor as "the greatest Warr Chief they have amongst them," is one example. The Bras Cassé, a Cree trading chief who was ceremonially clothed when he appeared at the fort, was treated with the same respect at Fort Chipewyan in 1800. The English Chief, a name which can be traced to 1821 at least (though it may not always refer to the same individual), is familiar from Alexander Mackenzie's account of his first voyage.

The spring trade at Athabasca reached its climax on 21 April, when the English Chief and the Old Chief arrived with about forty men. Thereafter, most of the trading was with Crees (and perhaps Chipewyans) who were hunting in the locality, and would sell moose and caribou carcasses to Pond and his men. A further important Chipewyan, the Big Chief's son-in-law from "the other side of Arabasca," appeared at the fort as late as 6 May, while the last trading encounter mentioned in the Journal, with an Indian called The Hand, took place after the brigade had left the fort, on 11 May.

Apart from the trade, the activities described in the Journal are the packing of furs, the making of pemmican, and the building of canoes. Canoe making was the responsibility of Charles Boyer, one of the clerks, and required the collection of suitable birch bark at "the Mountain" and the "Rivière au Hallier" – probably the Birch Mountains west of the fort and a river flowing from them. Pemmican was made in *taureaux* or skin bags, but, since little of the meat obtainable at Pond's post seems to have been buffalo (only two buffalo are mentioned in the Journal and most of the animals traded from Indian hunters were moose), it is possible that this pemmican was the variety made from dried fish as described by Mackenzie.[40] The fur proceeds of the season – 162 packs of eighty-eight pounds each, plus four robes and seventy-five skins traded on the way – were perhaps typical of early Athabasca, but still a very large number for a single post. The eight canoes despatched with the furs, at a typical lading of 22 packs per canoe, would have been just adequate for their burdens.

An unwelcome source of excitement was the flooding of the fort between 30 April and 3 May, because of ice jams in the Athabasca River. The Journal gives a vivid picture of this anxious time, with the men and the furs up in the garrets of the house, four feet of water over the floor, the floorboards rising, and the firewood and garden fence washing away. The susceptibility of the Old Establishment to spring flooding would have been one consideration in the move to the first Fort Chipewyan site in 1788.

On 6 May two senior canoemen, Piché and Rapin, appeared at the Fort from Île-à-la-Crosse with a letter for Peter Pond from the English River master, Patrick Small. A letter at such a time, when all of the efforts were directed at sending off the canoes with the season's trade, would have been very unusual, and it is probable that Small had learned some new information about the plans of the New Concern, and that the letter explained arrangements for sending two extra canoe loads of Île-à-la-Crosse goods up to Athabasca. Alexander Mackenzie was in charge for the New Concern at English River at this time, and one recalls his warning to his cousin Roderick the next year, no doubt based on experience, not to tell any of his plans to his voyageurs, for fear that men belonging to the North West Company would find them out in conversation.[41]

Peter Pond did not accompany the Athabasca brigade out in the spring of 1786, but remained inland for the summer. The first canoe left the fort on 7 May, six left the next day, and the last, containing Cuthbert Grant, departed on the 9th. The landmarks on the voyage are clearly given in the Journal, and almost all are familiar from later descriptions of the route. The brigade camped at the entrance of the Clearwater (the "little river") on the 14th, reached the north end of Portage La Loche on the 22nd, and finished the portage on the morning of the 28th. Here Pond and Patrick Small had intended that two canoe loads of goods would have arrived from Île-à-la-Crosse, and to save carrying canoes the two oldest of the Athabasca craft had been left on the north end of the portage. The Île-à-la-Crosse canoes did not appear, however, and Grant, finding himself with six canoes and eight ladings and crews, had to hire eight men at 100 *livres* per man to return across the portage and bring the two old canoes after all. The men made the round trip in less than twenty-four hours, and after gumming the canoes the brigade set off at once. The Journal ends with an entry made on the afternoon of 31 May, with the brigade wind-bound near the foot of the present Churchill Lake. From one of the inventories later in the English River Book, however, it is clear that they met the two canoes from Île-à-la-Crosse later on the 31st, and that Alexis Derry was sent to Athabasca with these canoes, while the brigade proceeded to Île-à-la-Crosse fort and arrived there on 1 June.[42]

Cuthbert Grant and the brigade seem to have left Île-à-la-Crosse for Lac La Pluie on 4 June,[43] and, since the accounts of the men with Mr Baldwin, the clerk at Rat River, were closed on 13 June, the brigade probably met Baldwin near Namew Lake on that date. No notice of their passage was taken in the summer journal of the Hudson's Bay Company post at Cumberland House, kept by George Hudson.[44]

The Trading Season of 1786–7

The Journal shows that Peter Pond intended to send men to Peace River under Charles Boyer and to Great Slave Lake under Alexis Derry to establish trading forts for the next season. These settlements presumably were made. In the fall of 1786 Cuthbert Grant, back from Grand Portage, took a further supply of goods to Great Slave Lake, and on this voyage two canoes, five men, and "some packages" were lost at the rapids on Slave River still called the Rapids of the Drowned.[45] Grant's house on Great Slave Lake was on the south shore, several miles east of the Slave River delta; Laurent Leroux, John Ross's clerk, built a house alongside in opposition.[46] It is quite likely that Ross also sent a party in opposition to Boyer at Peace River, but we have no evidence.

The crucial event of the 1786–7 trading season was the killing of John Ross. The available information about this incident is well known, and, as with Waddens' death, Peter Pond's guilt is unclear. Dr Bigsby's account, which he apparently had from David Thompson in 1817, implicates Pond as follows: "He persuaded his men to rob Mr. Ross of a load of furs in open day. In the course of the altercation Mr. Ross was shot, really by accident, from a gun in the hand of a *voyageur* named Péché."[47] Philip Turnor met a man who was evidently Piché at Great Slave Lake in 1791 (he does not name him), and according to Turnor "the dispute was about some Chepawyans as they were comming to the Houses to trade P Pond and his men being more numerous than Mr Rosses they were taking the Indians by force which Mr Ross opposed and in the dispute was shot."[48] Piché is listed in the English River Book, and his career in the Athabasca district may be traced for another twenty years.

A well-known passage in Roderick McKenzie's reminiscences records how the news of Ross's death was brought to English River by the Athabasca brigade in June 1787, and Roderick went to Grand Portage himself to report the "misfortune" to his employers. By his account, immediately upon receiving the news, the North West Company and the New Concern decided to amalgamate "for their common welfare." Alexander Mackenzie was sent to take charge of Athabasca, "where M. Pond, from the unfortunate circumstances of the preceding winter, had remained under a cloud."[49]

Pond appears to have passed part of the summer of 1787 exploring Great Slave Lake, for his map dated July 1787, which he prepared for presentation to the Empress of Russia, shows details of the lake, such as the North Arm and the correct location of the outlet to Mackenzie River at the west end, unlikely to have been obtained simply from Indian report. The map includes the notation, in the island-filled eastern arm, "much Ice July 1787," a detail which also sounds like personal observation.[50]

The relationship between Peter Pond and Alexander Mackenzie at Athabasca during the winter of 1787–8 can only be a subject for speculation. Isaac Ogden, at Quebec in the fall of 1789, was told by

Pond that he had left a "man by the name of McKenzie... at Slave Lake with orders to go down the River, and from thence to Unalaska, and so Kamskatsha, and then to England through Russia &c.[51] This sounds as though Mackenzie were acting under Pond's instructions, but Mackenzie's own account of his voyage of 1789 shows that he had to find the outlet of Mackenzie River on his own, approaching it by a roundabout route involving the North Arm and the north shore of Great Slave Lake. Even a glance at Pond's 1787 map would probably have saved Mackenzie several days, and it seems possible that Pond did not share all his knowledge with his young successor.

Pond left Athabasca and the northwest for good in the spring of 1788 and went down to Montreal. It would have been galling for him to know that the development of Athabasca would be entrusted by the North West Company almost entirely to former associates of John Ross and their relations. Besides the Mackenzies – Alexander himself, Roderick (who built Fort Chipewyan), Daniel, and James – the expansion of the trade into Peace River and the Great Slave Lake region in the late 1780s and 1790s was supervised by such men as Laurent Leroux, Ross's clerk, and John Finlay and Alexander McLeod, son and nephew, respectively, of two of John Gregory's sometime partners.

The name of Pond did appear in Athabasca again. One Augustin Peter Pond, of Sorel, was hired by McTavish, Frobisher and Company on 11 January, 1798, to go to the northwest,[52] and was posted to Fort Chipewyan, where he witnessed several hiring contracts, signing his own name, during the season of 1798–9. He signed his own two-year contract on 26 April, 1799, to work as "milieu & forgeron" at Fort Chipewyan or Rivière de la Paix.[53] Since Dr Bigsby, quoting information obtained from David Thompson, says that Peter Pond's son was "lately a blacksmith in Lower Canada,"[54] it is evident that Augustin, the *forgeron* of Fort Chipewyan, was Peter Pond's son. Augustin Pond remained in the North West Company's employment in Athabasca through the period 1811–21, and to judge from his salary he was a fairly senior man during those years. He was taken over by the Hudson's Bay Company at union in 1821 but was found to be "a poor workman at best"; he was retired to Canada with the pitifully small credit balance of 24 *livres* 6 *sous*, in 1822.[55] Thereafter he disappears.

THE ENGLISH RIVER ACCOUNT BOOK

The English River Book contains as its principal item the accounts of ninety-seven men. It is set up in standard double-entry form, with amounts due to the company of left-hand pages, and amounts to be paid the men on right-hand pages. In the present edition, the two halves of each account have been printed one above the other. For seventy-six of the men, balances, either credit or debit (mostly the former) were carried over from the accounts of 1784–5, which had been closed on 29 July, 1785 and do not survive. This date falls in the period during which the English River brigades would have reached Lac La Pluie (now Rainy Lake), the easternmost point on their annual voyage,[56] and so the detailed bookkeeping for 1784–5 must have been done there, probably by a clerk sent up from Montreal. The 1785–6 accounts, on the other hand, were closed before the brigades had left English River – on 1 June 1786 for most of the men, and on the 13th for those who had wintered at Rat River – and thus it appears that a change in accounting arrangements had been introduced in 1785. It is tempting to suggest that Cuthbert Grant was sent to English River specifically to introduce the new procedures in the district, to increase control over expenditure and relieve the pressure on the Montreal accountants during the few days available in late July at Lac La Pluie and Grand Portage. William McGillivray, who later claimed that he had been the first English-speaking clerk to be hired by the North West Company (in 1784), may have introduced the same practice at Red River, his posting in 1785–6.[57]

The Account Book gives information on a variety of topics. First, it provides what is probably a complete list of the men actually employed by the North West Company in English River (including Athabasca) in 1785–6, plus the names of four or five men who were on the books from the previous season, but had not returned to the district. This list almost always includes the rank or *qualité* of a man, and in most cases his wintering post can be inferred because he had charges transferred to this master account from other "Books" kept at Athabasca, at Île-à-la-Crosse, at Lac La Ronge, and by Mr. Baldwin, whom we know from other evidence to have wintered in 1785–6 near the lower Churchill, in what was later called the Rat River country. The man's wages are usually given. In some cases the goods for which he was charged are itemized, so that we know the actual prices for some articles; usually, however, they are lumped together as "sundries." Other specified transactions in some accounts give oblique information, as tantalizing as it is informative, about various aspects of voyageur life.

Charges for goods were made at Lac La Pluie (on 6 or 7 August 1785, just before the brigades left for their wintering grounds), occasionally "on the Road," and at the wintering post. Many of the Athabasca men were also charged for smaller amounts of goods at Île-à-la-Crosse. Their commonest purchases there were tobacco (measured in fathoms) and a *brayette* or breechclout.

It is probable that a man's requirements of European goods for the season were obtained when possible at Lac La Pluie at the start of the inward voyage, where prices were relatively low,[58] and thereafter, going and coming, as much as possible at Île-à-la-Crosse, to avoid the substantial surcharge which must have prevailed at Athabasca. Those Île-à-la-Crosse 1786 prices that can be inferred from itemized accounts are shown in table 1. There are no comparable prices available for Athabasca itself, unless two apparent overcharges for tobacco, at 30 *livres* per fathom compared to 20 *livres* in most of the Île-à-la-Crosse accounts, are Athabasca prices.[59] From table 1, it appears that tobacco cost twenty *livres* per fathom at Île-à-la-Crosse, but only eight *livres* at Lac La Pluie, for a surcharge on this item of 150 per cent.[60] There is little indication that men's wages in the remote posts were adjusted to compensate for the high cost of European goods at those points. Charles Boyer, the senior clerk at Athabasca, had negotiated the unusual privilege of buying trade goods from the Athabasca stocks at Grand Portage prices (see his account, page 106).

The Athabasca men, as a group, incurred much larger debts than did those stationed at Île-à-la-Crosse. Of the forty-four men showing debts transferred from the "Arabasca Book" in 1786, half owed more than 460 *livres*; of the thirty-four indebted only at Île-à-la-Crosse, half owed less than 183 *livres*. The individual amounts varied widely, of course – at Athabasca debts as small as 10 *livres* and as large as 1382 *livres* are recorded – but the trend is clear. This difference cannot be explained completely by surcharge on trade goods sold at Athabasca, relative to prices at Île-à-la-Crosse; another contribution to the high Athabasca debts may have been the fact that

TABLE 1
Prices of Trade Goods at Île-à-la-Crosse, 1786

Goods	Price
Ammunition 4 measures	16 *livres*
2 measures powder & ball	16 or 24 *livres*
Beads 75 "banches" & 1 doz rings	28 *livres*
Brayette (breechclout)	12
Calumet	6
Capot (size not specified)	40
Fire Steel	2
Gartering, piece	30
Gun	125
Hat	20
with 1 pair of shoes	35
Knife, small	4
large	6
"couteau resort"	5
cartouche	6
buck hand clasp[g]	5
Mantle, calamanco	20
Skins, orignal (dressed moose skin)	10 or 12
Strouds, per fathom	30
Tobacco, per fathom	20 or 30

Source: Compiled from the English River Account
     Book.

Note: It is suggested in the text that the price of
     30 *livres* per fathom for tobacco was actually
     an Athabasca price, charged by mistake. At
     Lac La Pluie, tobacco was 8 *livres* per fathom;
     see Pierre Duvalle's account, page 29.

the Athabasca men seem to have been longer in the service and
therefore more likely to have had Indian wives and children to
provide for. In the accounts of two of the Athabasca men, Joseph
Preux and François Raimond, charges were made for "passage of
your Woman," perhaps so that she could join her relations elsewhere in the district while her husband was away for the summer —
although it is also possible that these families were retiring to Canada. Charles Boyer's purchase of a boy's shirt, charged to his account,

suggests that he had at least one child with him in Athabasca, and Joseph Landry's purchase of "75 Banches [bunches] Beads & 1 doz Rings" at Île-à-la-Crosse in June 1786, listed in his account, may have been for his wife. Laprise, Lafleur, and Brousseau all had children who probably were born about 1786 if not before, a fact which suggests that they had established families about the time the English River Book was written. Laprise would have been one of the first voyageurs to take a Chipewyan wife.

The wages of the men seem to have reflected both their experience and their responsibilities. Four men are styled *commis* or clerk in the accounts, and two of those whose ranks are unstated (Primeau and Lesieur) are also known to have been clerks. The salaries of these six clerks ranged widely. Charles Boyer, who was probably the most experienced, and was also the canoe builder at Athabasca, had a salary of 1000 *livres* per annum, plus the rare privilege, already noted, of buying Athabasca trade goods at Grand Portage prices. Tourangeau, another clerk, had 800 *livres*, and Alexis Derry had 600. Paul Primeau, who was entering his second year of service in 1785, had 400 *livres*, and Jurial Baldwin had only 360 *livres*, calculated as equal to £30 Halifax currency.[61] Baldwin was probably hired as a writer and petty accountant and was not expected to be a skilful trader as yet. Although there is an account for Toussaint Lesieur, his salary is not listed and was perhaps kept private. There is no account for Cuthbert Grant.

Of the canoemen, the two guides – one for Athabasca, one for Île-à-la-Crosse – were in charge of directing their brigades in and out of the northwest, through the maze of the Churchill River; each received 1000 *livres* per annum. Most of the *devants* (bowsmen) and *gouvernails* (steersmen), collectively known as *bouts* (ends) received 800 *livres*. The wages for *milieux* (midmen, or common labourers) ranged from 290 to 550 *livres*. The most frequent *milieu*'s wage was 500 *livres* at Île-à-la-Crosse and 550 *livres* at Athabasca, perhaps indicating a slight premium for the longer distance (and higher prices) at the latter post.

Most of the canoemen had large debts on the books, a phenomenon frequently noted by critics of the Canadian fur trade. What is not so familiar is the practice, at least for valuable men, of forgiving parts of these debts as an inducement to rehire. Peter Pond, according to the Account book, used this method in persuading seven Athabasca men to accept new three-year contracts. Four of these men were *bouts*; one (Charles Papan), to judge by his wages, was an experienced *milieu*; and two (Nasplette and Mayotte) were perhaps interpreters. Some of the debts forgiven were quite substantial; in the case of Nasplette, it was more than a full year's wages.[62]

In a few cases, payments to particular men are noted for specified extra work. Joseph Landry and François Bouché were each credited with 100 *livres* for carrying canoes in the Portage La Loche – this must refer to the incident in the Journal entry of 28 May although eight men were actually hired and the others' payments may have been taken in kind. Five men, Laprise, Jean-Marie and François Bouché, Larivière, and Lalonde, each received 100 *livres* for a "voyage to Arabasca." Two of these were *devants*, one a *gouvernail*, and the other two experienced *milieux*, and it is probable that they were last-minute reinforcements for Athabasca from among the Île-à-la-Crosse men, sent in response to the appearance of John Ross. Joseph Guyette d'Yamaska had an additional 200 *livres* for a "voyage to Arabasca in the winter," probably carrying a letter from Patrick Small to Peter Pond; he, too, was added to the Athabasca strength. Cartier, one of the *devants* at Île-à-la-Crosse, was paid 191 *livres* for getting bark and mending canoes, while Messier, another Île-à-la-Crosse man, earned 100 *livres* extra for "fishing and mend^g of netts." Janvier Mayotte sold 50 beaver skins to the Athabasca establishment for 270 *livres*, duly credited to his account; this entry seems to set the money price of beaver there at 5 *livres* 8 *sous* in 1786. Fourteen other Athabasca men had amounts to their credit in the Athabasca book at the end of the season, in addition to their wages. Doubtless these credits were payments for extra services, for furs which they or their families had trapped, for prepared skins, moccasins or snowshoes which their wives had made, and so forth. These extra credits averaged 137 *livres* 10 *sous*, but varied between 16 and 458 *livres*. The largest amounts were those credited to Saint-Germain, the guide (458 *livres*), Laviolette (400 *livres*), and Piché (310 *livres*). Few Île-à-la-Crosse men were credited with extra income; perhaps there was more opportunity for extra duties at the more remote post.

Since there was no ready money in English River, any cash transactions had to be handled by appropriate transfers between men's accounts, and there are about two dozen of these. In a few cases the transactions are recorded in both men's accounts, but not always, and it must be assumed that, when a payment is not specifically listed, it was included among the "sundries" so often mentioned. Debts from the season of 1784–5 were discharged in some cases when the debtor bought his creditor goods at Lac La Pluie. The reason for a money transfer is rarely given – those few that are mentioned were purchases of skins, or clothes, or in one case a gun. Some transactions may have arisen when one man hired another to cut his quota of firewood (this was one of the few contracted duties of a voyageur upon reaching his wintering ground); gambling debts are another possibility. One pathetic entry is found in the account of François Lafrance, who died at Île-à-la-Crosse in the summer of 1785: it is credited with 31 *livres* on 26 February 1786, money paid by Joseph Durrocher and François Nadot, who had bought the dead man's clothes.

When money had to be sent to Canada, drafts or pay orders of various kinds were used. The North West Company directly paid small sums for J.B. Saint-Pierre to his mother, and for Nicholas Laliberté to his wife, both presumably in Canada. Seven accounts mention "drafts" prepared by Patrick Small, for amounts varying between 50 and 550 *livres*, no doubt for transmission to Canada. In addition, payments were made on behalf of Antoine Pagé and François Faniant to Joseph Faniant at Grand Portage on 3 August 1786; on behalf of Bonavan Parisien to one Tranchemontagne on 6 August 1786; and on behalf of Ambroise Lalonde to Basile Irelande on 21 September 1786. Joseph Faniant or Faignan and Basile Irelande were guides for the Montreal brigades which brought the goods up to Grand Portage, and returned with the furs, and Tranchemontagne was probably a Grand Portage guide as well (see their biographies in appendix B for the evidence). These transactions suggest that the guides might act as financial agents for voyageurs in the Upper Country.

Once the English River brigades reached Lac La Pluie, the Account Book evidently was handed over to an accountant at the depot, where missing items, such as the debts incurred by new men as they had come up from Montreal the previous summer, were filled in, and a few further transactions recorded. These additions are all in a different hand, which looks like that of Joseph Frobisher and indeed two are initialled "J.F." Once the additions had been made, the book, including the Journal which was part of it, would have returned to Montreal. Each man's account is initialled "J.H.," perhaps for James Hallowell, who had business dealings with Simon McTavish during the 1780s and became a partner of McTavish, Frobisher and Company, Montreal agents for the North West Company, in 1787.

THE ENGLISH RIVER ESTABLISHMENT, 1785–6

Of the ninety-seven men named in the Account Book, ninety were actually in English River in 1785–6.[63] At least seventy-two of these men had also been in the district in 1784–5, for their accounts were carried over from that season, and at least fourteen were newly arrived from Montreal. Not all the new arrivals were novices – they included two *gouvernails* and one *devant*, plus one man, Piccott, whose rank is not specified but was also entrusted with a *devant*'s responsibilities. Doubtless these veterans had spent a year or more down in Canada, and were returning for a further tour of duty in the Upper Country.

Table 2 lists all the men assigned to the different English River posts, with their ranks and wages. Forty-eight men were assigned to Athabasca (plus Cuthbert Grant and Pond himself), thirty to Île-à-la-Crosse (plus Patrick Small), five to Lac La Ronge, and seven, including Jurial Baldwin, to Baldwin's post in the Rat River region. Except for Lac La Ronge, which was probably operated as an outpost from Île-à-la-Crosse, not open in the summer, the numbers of *devants* and *gouvernails* at each post are about the same (exactly the same if the complement at Lac La Ronge is combined with that of Île-à-la-Crosse, and guides are counted as *devants*). There are slightly more than twice as many *milieux* as *devants* or *gouvernails*. These numbers confirm that the crew of a north canoe was four, two *bouts* and two *milieux*. The extra *milieux* in each district would be summer men, who remained at the posts while the rest were away on the long voyage to and from the summer rendezvous. The complement of men for Athabasca included ten *gouvernails*, and nine *devants* plus the guide. As the Journal shows, eight canoes were sent out with the furs in May 1786, which would have left the crews of two canoes, plus two more canoes sent up from Île-à-la-Crosse at the end of May, for the summer expeditions to build posts at Peace River and Great Slave Lake. The posts of Île-à-la-Crosse and Lac La Ronge together had six *gouvernails* and five *devants* plus the guide, for a maximum of six canoes (of which two went to Athabasca in May). Baldwin had one canoe's crew with him plus two summer men.

TABLE 2
The North West Company's English River Establishment, 1786

Rank or qualité	Athabasca (wages in livres)	Île-à-la-Crosse (wages in livres)	Lac La Ronge (wages in livres)	Rat River (wages in livres)
guides	St Germain, P (1000)	Monette, F (1000)	–	–
devants (bowsmen)	Bouché, JM (800)	Aussan, P (800)	Leblanc, F (800)	Letendre, JB (800)
	Caesar, H (800)	Cartier, J (800)	Pagé, A (800)	
	Duvalle, P (800)	Parisien, B (800)		
	Larivière, F (800)			
	Martin, S (800)			
	Piché, F (800)			
	Preux, J (800)			
	Raimond, F (900)			
	*Rapin, JB(800)			
gouvernails (steersmen)	Bellanger, P (800)	Antaya, JB (800)	–	Guyette, C (800)
	Bodoin, B (800)	Cardinal, J (800)		
	Bruilette, P (800)	Durrocher J (800)		
	Derry, J (800)	Fortin, L (800)		
	Faniant, F (800)	Lavallé, I (800)		
	Jolybois, F (800)	Lavallé, JB (800)		

Rank or qualité	Athabasca (wages in livres)	Île-à-la-Crosse (wages in livres)	Lac La Ronge (wages in livres)	Rat River (wages in livres)
	*Lalonde, A (800)			
	Landrieffe, J (800)			
	Landry, J (800)			
	Quisson, – (800)			
milieux (midmen)	Bouché, F (650)	Babeu, E (500)	*Aubuchon, F (390)	Gagnier, JB (550)
	Brisbois, L (450)	Bourcier, A (500)	*Constantino, N (350)	Leuneau, JM (500)
	Brousseau, L (800)	Boyé, A (500)	*Laliberté, N (400)	*Modeste, A (400)
	Brunosh, JB (450)	*Bruno, JB (400)		
	Deveau, C (500)	Coté, L (500)		
	*Doucette, C (550)	Forcier, J (500)		
	Duchain, J (300)	Guy, JB (500)		
	Dumas, P (500)	*Lacharité, P (390)		
	Durrell, F (550)	Messier, C (500)		
	Guyette, J (550)	Nadot, F (390)		
	Lafleur, JB (400)	*Papan, J (500)		
	Languedoc-que, JB (500)	Preux, P (500)		
	Laprise, JB (500)	Réaume, S (500)		
	Laverdure, J (550)	*?St-Pierre, JB (300)		
	Laviolette, F (550)	Vertifeuille, J (300)		

Rank or qualité	Athabasca (wages in livres)	Île-à-la-Crosse (wages in livres)	Lac La Ronge (wages in livres)	Rat River (wages in livres)
	Ledoux, D (550)			
	Maranda, J (500)			
	Marcille, P (500)			
	Papan, C (550)			
	Perrault, J (550)			
	Scavoyard, JB (500)			
	Thesson, JB (350)			
commis or clerks	Boyer, C (1000) Derry, A (600)	Tourangeau, A (800)	–	Baldwin, J (360)
unspecified	Guyette, J (500) Mayotte, J (600) Nasplette, J (550) *Piccott, A (350)	De Raimond, P (300) Lesieur, T (?) *Mayé, P (375) *Roy, P (400)		Primeau, P (400)
others, not in Account Book	Grant, Cuthbert Pond, Peter	Small, Patrick		

Source: Compiled from the English River Account Book.

* Not in English River, 1784–5.

The lists of men assigned to the various posts show that the experienced men were concentrated at Athabasca. Only six of the forty-eight men in this district had not been in English River the preceding year, and all of the new arrivals (marked with asterisks in table 2) had previous experience to judge by their wages or other criteria (see appendix B for details). Of the thirty-five men at Île-à-la-Crosse and Lac La Ronge, on the other hand, eight were new arrivals whose wages were 400 *livres* or less, a level which suggests that they were novice canoemen. That all or most of the men assigned to Athabasca were experienced would be explained by the facts that the post was expanding into unknown territory, and that the competition with John Ross was taken seriously.

The names of the men who worked for the North West Company in English River in 1785–6 are of more than routine interest because in some respects they were an élite. The North West Company had only recently been organized in a permanent form, and, in the English River district in particular, the company was about to commence a period of expansion which did not falter for twenty-five years. In 1786, prompted by the competition of the New Concern as we have seen, posts were to be established up the Beaver River from Île-à-la-Crosse, and on Peace River and Great Slave Lake from Athabasca. This was only the beginning. The first post on the Mackenzie River itself was built in 1796, and the network had been extended to the full length of that river and its major tributaries by 1810. From Peace River, the company had spread its operations over the Rocky Mountains into New Caledonia, the upper valley of the Fraser, soon after 1805. Although the talent available to the company for these expansions was continually improved by a series of takeovers and amalgamations with competitors, in a surprising number of cases the men of the English River Book of 1786 are found playing major roles in the expansions.

This conclusion can be reached only by considering the individual careers of the ninety-seven men listed in the English River Book, as is done in appendix B. Almost half of the names in the list are otherwise unknown, and some of these doubtless spent only a few years in the North West Company's service. Of those who can be identified with some confidence, a few were veterans of the fur trade of New France. Pierre Marcille and Augustin Piccott both seem to have been pre-Conquest voyageurs – Piccott was a part of the last expedition to be sent under the Old Régime to the *poste de l'Ouest*, then under the command of Dejordy de Villebon. Paul Saint-Germain, the Athabasca guide known as "Buffalo Head," was born about 1737 and so is likely to have entered the fur trade before the Conquest; he was in the Athabasca country from the time the district was opened to the trade, and remained there until his death early in 1804. François Monette, the Île-à-la-Crosse guide in 1786, may be the man of this name who was born in Montreal in 1718, making him sixty-seven years old in 1786. This man was married to the aunt of Jean-Baptiste Rapin, one of the English River *devants*, and through this marriage was related to a number of voyageurs and fur traders of Lachine in the pre-Conquest period.

No fewer than fifteen of the English River canoemen of 1786 are known to have served the North West Company later as interpreters and sometimes *commis*, growing grey in the service.[64] The names of Simon Réaume and Joseph Cartier are familiar at English River itself, while Lafleur and Brousseau are frequently mentioned at Peace River and Piché and Laprise were involved in the expansion into the Mackenzie Valley. Several of these men seem to have retired just after the coalition with the XY Company, but of the twelve interpreters listed for Athabasca for 1806–7, six were still English River Book names, and another was the son of one of these six.[65] Most of these had retired by 1811, when the North West Company's surviving great ledger of men's accounts, HBCA F.4/32, begins. As many as twelve of the English River Book men, however, seem to be in this ledger (although many of the identifications can only be tentative), and of those twelve, six were taken over by the Hudson's Bay Company in 1821. All but one of the remaining six were retired as a result of George Simpson's decisive reduction in manpower in 1822.[66] The last survivor in the service was Joseph Cartier, who had transferred from English River to the Columbia Department in 1813, and served there until his retirement to Canada in 1827, when he was in his early seventies and had spent more than fifty-five years in the northwest fur trade.

The Journal names seven men who were hired to winter at Peace River, beginning with the season of 1786–7, and thirteen who were to winter at Great Slave Lake (table 3). Of these thirteen, six certainly (Doucette, Landry, Laverdure, Laprise, Passpartout, and Perrault) and two probably (Dumas and Laviolette) are mentioned in records

TABLE 3
Men Hired for Peace River and Great Slave Lake, April 1786

Peace River	Great Slave Lake
Charles Boyer	Alexis Derry; Cuthbert Grant
"Old Joseph" [perhaps Joseph Duchain] – hired 7 Apr	Joseph Landry Cadien – hired 3 Apr
Goyette – 10 Apr	Charles Doucette Cadien – 3 Apr
Caesar – 12 Apr	Ledoux – 3 Apr
Pierish [Pierre Duvalle] – 12 Apr	Laprise – 3 Apr
Deveau – 13 Apr	Perrault – 3 Apr
Lafleur – 14 Apr	Laviolette – 3 Apr
Papan – 14 Apr	Landrieffe – 7 Apr
	Laverdure – 7 Apr
	Dumas – 7 Apr
	Brisbois – 7 Apr
	Passpartout – 7 Apr
	Scavoyard – 7 Apr
	Joseph Derry – 24 Apr

Source: Compiled from the English River Journal.

Note: Square brackets indicate tentative identifications; see further appendix B, under Joseph Duchain and Pierre Duvalle. Cadien means acadien.

after 1786, but five have not been traced. These five – Brisbois, Joseph Derry, Landrieffe, Ledoux, and Scavoyard – may well be the five voyageurs who perished at the Rapids of the Drowned in Slave River, in the fall of 1786, while taking Cuthbert Grant's expedition to Great Slave Lake (see page xxii, above).

Among the Great Slave Lake men who did survive this accident were perhaps the two best-known voyageurs. Joseph Landry and Charles Doucette, the two Cadiens at Athabasca in 1785–6, were probably cousins, members of Acadian families which had settled at Sorel after the expulsion from Acadia. These two were among the four canoemen who took Alexander Mackenzie to the Arctic Ocean and back in the summer of 1789. Four years later they were among the seven who carried him on his immortal journey to the Pacific.

PERSONALITIES IN THE ENGLISH RIVER BOOK

In appendix A I have listed all the Indians mentioned by name in the English River Book Journal, and given other information about them when I have found it. Only one, the English Chief, is well known (see also Sloan, 1987), but several others are mentioned in Athabasca documents almost twenty years later. In appendix B I have attempted biographies of all the English River Book voyageurs, clerks and traders, and a few other individuals mentioned in the book and not discussed elsewhere. One of the latter is the neglected figure, John Cornelius Vandriel, whom Alexander Mackenzie credits with the first survey of Peace River.

THE
ENGLISH
RIVER
BOOK

CONTENTS

of the original edition

Page numbers of the original edition are
shown in italic, with those for this edition given
at the right.

CREE TRADING

VOCABULARY

On the first page of the English River Book is the following list of Indian words. It is untitled, and was evidently compiled for the use of a trader. In his biography, it is suggested that Cuthbert Grant, the keeper of the English River Book Journal, collected the words for his own use. Almost all the words can be found in Cree vocabularies provided by Isham (Rich, 1949), Graham (Williams, 1969), Alexander Mackenzie (1801), Alexander Henry the younger (Coues, 1965), and Harmon (1973). Isham's and Graham's vocabularies were collected from Indians trading at Churchill and York Factory, in the 1740s and 1760s, respectively; Henry's at Red River and on the Saskatchewan, between 1799 and 1812; Harmon's in the Swan River district, at Cumberland House, and in various other parts of the northwest, between 1800 and 1811; and Mackenzie's, between 1785 and 1793, at English River or Athabasca itself. Of the words in the list, the only examples not found in any of the five vocabularies consulted are the two words for gartering, *Masiniquachiganeabe* and *Aquachigan*, and *Caskiquachiganeabe*, one of the words for thread. Two of these words are evidently compounds with the familiar Cree word *shaganappe*, a string or thong, while the third, *Aquachigan*, seams to be a shorter form of the first; and less unwieldy words would have developed as the Indians became more familiar with these items.

Maniteuegin[1], Strouds
Wabawoyan[2], a Blanket
Caskite[3] ⎫
         ⎬ Pouder
Pichkaw[4] ⎭
Mossasinie[5], Balls
Niscasinie[6], Shote
Assasoui[7], an Ice Trench
Miwite[8], a flatte Do
Chigayigan[9], an axe
Kiskiman[10], a fille
Assesian[11], a Bryette

Naquoy[12], a Pair Sleeves
Misqutagay[13] ⎫ a Capote
         ⎬ a Shirte
Masiniquachiganeabe[14] ⎫
Aquachigan[15] –   ⎬ Gartering
Caskiquachiganeabe[16] ⎫
Assabap[17] –   ⎬ Thread
Achanich[18] – Rings
Chageheigan[19], a flint
Caskquakinagan[20], a Tobaco Box

NOTES ON CREE VOCABULARY

1 *Man tu ig gan*, cloth (Isham, in Rich, 1949, 39); *Manetoweguin*, cloth (Mackenzie, 1801, cxii); *Manitouhaigan*, strouds (Henry, in Coues, 1965, 537); *Mon-ne-too-wa-gen*, cloth (Harmon, 1973, 342).

2 *Wap pa wi an*, blankets (Isham, 39); *Wapewean*, blanket (Graham, in Williams, 1969, 208); *Wape weyang*, blanket (Mackenzie, cxii); *Wahpewwian*, blanket (Henry, 537); *Wa-bo-e-un*, blanket (Harmon, 337).

3 *Kur ske tau*, powder (Isham, 38); *Kusketaien*, powder (Henry, 537); *Kus-ke-ta*, powder (Harmon, 343).

4 *Pe co*, powder (Isham, 38); *Pecu*, gunpowder (Graham, 207).

5 *Moo su si nee*, "low Et. India shott or moase [moose] shott" (Isham, 39); *Moosassinni*, ball (Henry, 537); *Mo-sus-se-nu*, balls (Harmon, 343).

6 *Nish ko ar si nee*, "Bristow Shott or Grey goose shott" (Isham, 38); *Nis-cus-se-ne-uck*, shot (Harmon, 343). Evidently a compound of *-assinni*, "shot of sorts; a stone" (Graham, 207) with the word for a kind of goose, *Neish cock* ("a Grey goose," Isham, 23), *Niscag* ("outard," Mackenzie, cix), etc.

7 *Arsisue*, "a Broad Ice chissel" (Isham, 40).

8 *Me wiss*, "a Narrow Ice chissel" (Isham, 40).

9 *Chi ka hig gan*, a hatchet (Isham, 40); *Chikahegan*, a hatchet (Graham, 208); *Shegaygan*, an ax (Mackenzie, cx); *Chickahhoicun*, a hatchet (Henry, 537); *Chee-ki-e-gun*, axe (Harmon, 339).

10 *Kiskeman,* a file (Henry, 537).
11 *Ar se an,* "a Cloth for the private parts" (Isham, 14); *As-si-an,* breech cloth (Harmon, 337).
12 *No qui,* a sleeve (Isham, 14).
13 *Muska togy,* "a tockey" or cloak (Isham, 14).
14 No equivalent found, but evidently a compound with *-shaga- nappe,* a string (Isham, 14).
15 No equivalent found, but apparently an abbreviated version of the last.
16 No equivalent found but see 14.
17 *Assabab,* thread (Mackenzie, cxii); *As-se-bâpe,* thread (Harmon, 342).
18 *At tu'n nish,* "Rings plaine" (Isham, 41); *Us-ton-is,* ring (Harmon, 337).
19 *Chaw ka she ig gan,* flints (Isham, 40); *Scoutecgan,* fire steel (Mackenzie, cx); *Schoutaikaun,* fire-steel (Henry, 537); *Chak-is- say-e-gun,* gun flint (Harmon, 340).
20 *Ar ske ko kin a kun,* tobacco boxes (Isham, 41).

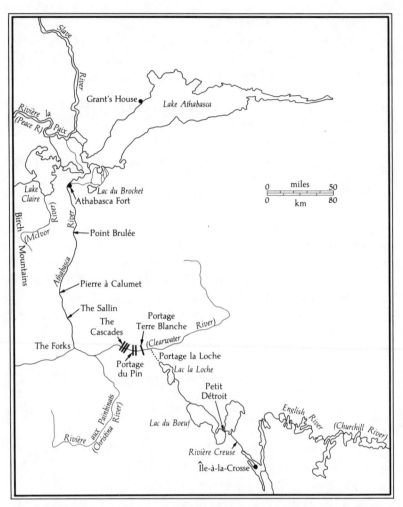

The English River district, 1786, showing the canoe route described in the English River Book. Names given are those used in that period, except for a few modern names which are in parentheses.

THE

JOURNAL

[p. 2]   1786. Arabasca[1] 1st April 1786 Saturday
This Morning the Bigg Chiefs Band[2] who Arrived
yesterday Traded about two packs[3] among twenty
men at midday one lodge of them went away after
Mr Pond had told them not to Come any more to this
Fort that Derry[4] Should go this Summer and build a
fort at the lack des Esclave[5] and that I would go there
next fall with the goods, at one O clock there Arrived
a young man from the old Chiefs Band for Tobaco[6]
he left them two days ago on the other Side of lack
[lake] Arabasca at four O'clock there Arrived a young
man from the Tittons[7] Chief of the Beaver Indians[8]
for Tobaco whom he left yesterday with Six men at
little lack Arabasca[9] at the Same time arrived Six
Crees two of which is of the Beaver River Indians[10]
and has never been here before they are Come from
war and has Brougt in a Sleave [slave] –

Sunday 2nd This Morning the Achibawayans[11] ["Sam
that passed the winter" is written above the line] has
Treaded [traded] about two more Packs at 10 Oclock
the Titton Arrived with his band and they paid there
Credit[12] Imediately, about 4 PM Oclock the Achiba-
wayans Began to Drink[13] & Soon after the Beaver
Indians & Crees Joined them & they Continue Still to
Drink Treading Skins and Provisions[14] Derry Treads

with them in Mr Ponds Kitchen as he Chose that Derry Should Tread rather than Boyer[15] or me – Munday 3rd fine weather all day with light wasterly [westerly] wind, the indians Traded in the night about 120 Skins and a little Provisions, and in the morning the Beaver Indians Treaded about 1½ Packs –

[p. 2d]   about 2 Oclock there Arived three Achibawayans from above and a little afterwards L'homme de Castor[16] arrived with 2 other Crees I Engaged the two Cadiens[17] Le Doux[18] La Prise[19] Perault[20] Laviolette[21] & Janvier[22] for three years all Except Janvier to winter at the Lack Des Esclave, in the afternoon I Equipt Janvier Brusseau[23] Faignan[24], Chales Cadien[25] & Duveau[26] to go for the Bark that Janvier raised last Summer in the Rivier au Hallier[27] – at 9 Oclock the old Blind Woman & her son arrived from the Shining Rock's Band[28] who is to Come to the Fort as soon as they raise the Bark for there Cannoes –

Teusday 4th This Morning Janvier, Brusseau, Cadien Faignain & Duveau went for the Bark, the Achibawayans that Arrived yesterday paid there Credit, one of the Beaver Indians who Treaded his Robe[29] when in Liquor wanted to get a Blanket or Capot[30] on Credit which Mr Pond Refused him he afterwards took a piece of Tobaco[31] & wanted to buy a robe from one of the Achibawayans but he would not Sell it oupon [upon] which he wanted to take it by force, the others was frightened & went for Mr Pond, who came and Cutt the Beaver Indian on the head with his Poinard, oupon which they told him it was the last time they ever Should see the fort, But he afterwards gave him a Blanket & some Amunition to appease him,[32] I tied 23 Beals [bales] of Skins,[33] & Mr Boyer made 4 Cannoe Maiters[34] – about 4 O clock the Beaver Indians went away

[p. 3]   Wedensday 5th Northerly wind with Cloudy weather all day & Cold about 10 o Clock there arrived two

Achibawayans from Lack de Brochet[35] with two trains of meat,[36] at 4 O Clock Savoyard[37] Arrivied from St Germain[38] with 15 fathom of Bark which he Raised at the Mountain,[39] St Germain Sent word that he was not Shour [sure] whether he could find any more or not Mr Pond made two Maitres de Medicine[40] Mr Boyer wanted to mak one also But Mr Pond told him that the Countery and Indians belonged to him & that he would do with them as he pleased & no other Person Should mudle with them – Mr Boyer made a Gabaric & two lieces[41] –

Thursday 6th North Wast wind Blowing fresh with thick snow & drift all day in the morning Laverdeure[42] & Mersille[43] arrived with the wood of the two Cannoes that was at the Lack[44] also Arrived from the lack La Bonne[45] Landrie[46] F. Bouché[47] Dumas,[48] about 2 O clock the Achibawayan Called the Boudar[49] Arrived with two others from above[50] the two that Arrived yesterday paid their Credit & Treaded a little meat, Mr Pond made another Manetre de Paix[51] –

Fraiday 7th Northwast wind all day the Achibawayans that Arrived yesterday treaded about a pack, Landriefe, Laverdeur, Dumas, Brisbois,[52] Passpartout[53] & Savoyard Engaged to winter 3 years at the lack des Esclave,[54] Old Joseph 3 years in the River la paix,[55] & La Bonne one year –

Saturday 8th Northerly wind & very Cold all day, our people had their allowance of fresh meat,[56] about 2 OClock the Carcajeau[57] & two other Crees Arrived from the other Side of Arabasca, they paid their Credit & Treaded a few Skinns –

[p. 3d] Sunday 9th North East wind with thick snow all day, about 10 O Clock the Achibawayan Called the Chantair[58] with two others Arrived from above, & at 2 O Clock St Germain Ceasar[59] & Langdeau[60] arrived from the Mountain with 14 fathoms of Bark which was all they Could find, La Grain & the Orriginial[61] killed four Carribeaux, Mr Pond Engaged Belleangé[62] for three years, the first year to stay in the Countery, & the other two to go to the Portage[63] –

Mounday 10th Westerly wind and Snow in the Morning about 10 O'Clock arrived one Achibawayan from Behinde the [sic] he paid his Credit immediately and Treaded a little Meat, at 6 OClock Arrived 2 young men from the English Chiefe,[64] Whome they left 3 Days ago with the Bigg Chief's son in law the old Chief that was with Derry,[65] the Chiefe Cancre[66] & Grand Piccotté,[67] in all 10 Lodges Comming to the fort but they say that they have but few peltries[68] Mr Boyer Engaged Goyette that Camme from the Isle la Cross[69] to winter in the River la paix

Teusday 11th. Cloudy weather and Westerly wind about 10 O Clock the two men that Came from the English Chiefe yesterday went away at 12 O'Clock the Rock qui Relouis[70] with five men Arived from Above they have not killed above one half their Credit, at 6 O clock arived two Achibawayans from above with some Originials flesh[71] that they killed yesterday one of the Crees that went a hunting this Morning killed an Originial and Brought Some of the flesh of it to Mr Pond,

Wedensday 12th Cloudy weather & Northerly wind all day about 4 O Clock Arrived 3 Crees from above, the Gendre[72] killd two Orriginials & two Beavers, one of the Orriginials he Sold to Mr Pond Mr Boyer Engaged Ceasar & Pierish[73] to winter 3 years in the Rivier la paix –

[p. 4]   Thursday 13th Cloudy weather alle day about 10 O Clock arrived to [two] Achibawayans from Below with some meat which they Treaded Immediately, at 12 O Clock the men Arrived with the Originial that the Gendere killed yesterday,[74] we saw Several Egles [eagles] today flying about the fort which is the first we saw this year, Mr Boyer Engaged Duveau for three years in the Rivier la Paix – Janvier, Brusseau, Faignan, Cadien & Duvaut,[75] arrived with the hundred and twenty fathons [fathoms] of Bark that Janvier raised in the Rivier au Hallier last Summer[76] –

Fraiday 14th Cloudy weather & Northerly wind Mr Boyer Engaged Lafleur[77] & Papain[78] to winter three years in the Rivier la Paix –

Saturday 15th Esterly wind & thick snow all day the Cree called the little Originial[79] killed an Originial & Sold it to Mr Pond, Cadien Laviollet & Bruilliete[80] went & Brought it to the fort –

Sunday 16th About 10 O Clock arrived an Indian from the English Chiefe for Tobaco he left them yesterday at the lack he says that they have very few Peltries and is going to stay two or three days at the lack to fish for Troute about 3 O Clock 3 Achibawayans [arrived] from above with Some Meat the Crees killed 2 Originials & sold one of them to Mr Pond, they are now Drinking –

Munday 17th About 8 O Clock the man that Came from the English Chiefe went away at 12 O Clock there Arrived three Achibawayans from Below they paid there Credits, the Indians Saw a Swan today which is the first that has been Seen this year the men Brought the originial that the Grain killed yesterday to the fort –

[p. 4d]   Tuesday April 18 fine warme weather & Sutherly wind we saw Several Geese & Ducks to day which is the first we saw this year about there [three] o clock there arrived three Achibawayans from Below they have Brouht nothing a little after arrived two Crees from the Bras Casser[81] whom they left at the Portage de pin[82] and is to Come here to Morow Mr Boyer went to inCampe at the little Ecore[83] for to make the Cannoes as we are afraid of the waters Raising here, Mr Pond sent two men to the little lake De poison Blanc to See if there was any part of it oppen for to send the men to live there, but they Returned with the news of its Being Still Shut up[84] –

Wensday 19 Cloudy weather & westerly wind all day in the morning there Arrived three Achibawayans from Below they say they have not seen the English Chiefe about 2 O Clock the Bras Casser & the Peccan[85] arrived from Above with two others they paid part of there Credit Mr Pond Clothed[86] the Bras Casser & they are now Drinking –

Thursday 20 Cloudy weather & northerly wind the Crees Treaded 80 Skins in the night,[87] about 10 O Clock the Bras Casser with 4 Lodges of the Crees went & Camped at the little Ecore to make their Cannoes, at 11 O clock there Arrived three Achiba-wayans from Bellow, they they [sic] say they did not see the English Chiefe, and we Suspect that the Big Chiefe Sent him word not to Comme to the fort but wait for Ross Below, Ross told the hand that he was one of the Hudsons Bay People and they Seem in General to believe it[88] Mr Pond Sent off Preux[89] with a pair of Couller[90] and some Tobaco and Amunition in Search of the English Chiefe –

[p. 5]   Fraiday 21 April Nortwast wind & Cold all day in the morning the Rest of the Crees went & Camped at the little Ecore to make their Cannoes, about 11 O Clock the English Chiefe Arrived with about 40 men with him Some of them paid their Credite & Mr Pond Clothed the English Chiefe & the old Chiefe that was with Derry this winter –

Saturday 22 Northerly wind & Cloudy weather all day Laverdeur, Dumas Jolybois[91] & Laland[92] went to the Lack de Poison Blanc, the Achibawayans Treaded a few Skins in the Evening it rained a little

Sunday 23 Sutherly & fine weather all day, the Achibawayans Treaded about 6 Packs to day, La Bonne Mersille Ceasar & Brisbois went to the lack De Poison Blanc, in the Evening one of the Crees Arrived with a Train load of Carribeau meat which he Treaded Bouché & La Rivier[93] Carried their Cannoe to the little Ecore to be made a new —

Munday 24 Sutherly wind with flying Clouds & Small Shwers [Showers] of Rain Martain[94] Lafleur & Brunosh[95] went a hunting to the little lack Arabasca, Mr Pond killed a Gouse flying over the fort, Bruilliet made a pair of Scails [scales] for weighing the packs,[96] I engaged Jos Derry[97] to winter three years at the lack Des Esclaves

Tusday 25 Sutherly wind & fine weather all day we made twenty Packs to day[98] Mr Boyer made the Beds for to make the Cannoes in[99] Picoté[100] Engaged for three years to winter at this place the two Bouchés

[p. 5d]   La Rivier Faignan Jos Derry Goyetté[101] Papan & Duveau went to the lack de poison Blance —

Wensday 26 Sutherly wind & fin [fine] weather till the afternoon when it Rained a little we made 30 packs to day Mr Boyer made[102] a new Cannoe, the Peltries Mr Boyer made last Summer[103] was made up to day which amounted to 30 Packs 88 lb English weight

Thursday 27 Sutherly wind & fine weather, Brisbois & Dumas Arrived from the little lack de poison Blanc, Brisbois brought 4 Geese for Mr Pond, we made 22 Packs to day —

Fraiday 28 Esterly wind & fine weather all day in the Morning Brisbois & Dumas went to the lack de poison

Blanc, about 12 O Clock the Ice began to Brack [break] up in the Rivier & Continues to mouve & Stop alternately, we made 28 Packs to day. Mr Pond killed a Gouse & I killed two Ducks. Mr Boyer made a new Cannoe –

Saturday 29 Northerly wind & fine weather all day the Ice keept going down the River till about 4 O clock in the afternoon when it stopt, the water is now almost on a levele with the Banks & we are obliged to keep a watch in Case it Should overflow the Banks, we made 30 Packs to day, the Graine killed 4 Geese & 1 Swan –

[p. 6]　Sunday 30 April North wast wind & Cold all day at one O clock in the morning the Ice made a Dame [dam] oposite to the fort & in less than ten minuts time we had 18 inches water in the fort, but it soon retired & about 8 o Clock it Began to rise again & soon retired Mr Pond left the for [fort] & went to Camp at the little Ecore at 12 the Ice Began to mouve again, & the water rose to the hight of 2 foot in the fort but the Ice soon Stopt again & the water retired again we put a number of loggs Before the fort for to Keep of [off] the Ice at four O Clock the water Began to rise again & we have now 18 inches in the fort all the People in the Garrets, & we keep a watch for fear of the Ice Braking in upon the fort –

Munday 1st May 1786 North wast wind & Cold all day at 8 o Clock the Ice Began to mouve & the water to fall, at 12 o Clock the Ice Stopt at the point Below the fort & in less than ½ an hour we had 4 feet water above the floor of the houses, & many large Pieces of Ice floating about the houses, all the wood Which Mr Pond had Squered [squared] & Drawn for to Build a house this Summer is gon a Drift & all the Garden fence,[104] all the loggs we put before the fort went a Drift also the partitions in Mr Ponds house raised part of the Garret flour [floor] –

[p. 6d]   Tuesday 2 May Northerly wind & Cold all day, at three O Clock in the Morning the Ice Began to move & the water fell 3 feet, at 8 the Ice Stoped Again & the water rose to the hight of 3 feet, at 12 O clock the Ice Began to move again, & at 4 O Clock it stoped at the point Below the for wher [fort where] it still remains, the Rivier is entirely Clear above the fort we have still 3 feet water in the houses —

Wedensday 3 Esterly wind & Cloudy weather with a little rain in the morning, at 6 O Clock the Ice gave way & at 8 the fort was dry, we imeadeatly set about laying the floors & putting the Houses to rights in the Evening we made 8 Toureaux of Pimitegan[105] the water has fallen 5 feet from 6 O Clock in the morning till nine at night —

Thursday 4th Northerly wind & Cold, in the morning Mr Pond Came Back to the fort, & Employed a Pacele [parcel] of Indians to Geather & put up his Garden fence gain [again] he sent Quison[106] to the lack de Poison Blanc for the people of 4 Cannoes which he proposes Sending off the day after tomorrow[107] Mr Boyer made the 4 Cannoe to day & I made 14 Toureaux of pimitigan the woman made a Barril of Gum[108] & St-Germain went to the little Arabaca to look for some of the men that has Gon a hunting there

[p. 7]   Fraiday 5 May Westerly wind & Cold in the morning at 12 O Clock all the men Exept 6 Arrived from the lack De poisson Blanc & in the afternoon we made 8 packs —

Saturday 6 Sutherly wind & fine weather, all the people Bussie [busy] in getting the Cannoes finishd. Mr Boyer Came to the fort after making 4 Cannoes at the little Eecore, Martain, Lafleur & Brunoch Arrived from the little Arabasca at 6 Oclock Piché[109] &

Rapain[110] Arrived from the Isle la Cross with a letter from Mr Small for Mr Pond, a little after the Bigg Chiefe's Son in law Arrived from from [sic] the other side of Arabasca he has not been at the fort this year before, we made 20 packs to day which is all we had to make, there is in all 160 Packs I Engaged Rapain for 3 years to Stay in the land –

Sunday 7th Sutherly wind & fine weather all day the Bigg Chiefe's son in law Treaded about 1½ pa' [packs] About 12 O Clock Preux's Cannoe[111] went off loaded with 22 packs, four of the men went & Brougt a Buffalo to the fort which the Bigg Chiefe's son in Law killed yesterday in the Island,[112] in the Evening Brisbois Arrived from the lack De poison Blanc –

[p. 7d]   Munday 8 May Wasterly wind & fine weather all day St Germains Martains La Rivier's Bouché's Picoté's Ceasar's Canoes[113] went off today, in the afternoon we made 2 Packs –

Tuesday 9 Northerly wind & Cold all day in the morning there arrived two men from the hand,[114] who Treaded a few Skins Mr Pond ordered me to leave the two old Canoes at this end of the Portage as he Expects the People from the Isle la Cross will be there before we are Don the Portage,[115] at 9 O Clock I left the fort in the last Canoe,[116] In the afternoon it Snowed a little we Camped about a leage below the point Brullie[117] – Pierish in hoisting the Sail threw my Gun overboard[118] –

Wensday 10 Northerly wind & very Cold at 6 O Clock we Came up with the Canoes at the point Brulle at 2 O Clock it Blew so hard with thick Snow & hard frost, that we was obliged to Camp 3 leags abouve the point Brullie –

Thursday 11 Northerly wind & hard frost with a little Snow in the morning at sun Set we came up with

Preuxs Canoe and the piere a Callimet[119] where
I found the hand[120] & three others Indians the rest
of the Canoes Camped 2 leags Below –

Fraiday 12 In the morning I treaded with the Indians
75 Skins & 4 Robs [robes][121] for which I gave them
Billets to be paid at Arabasca where the hand prom-
ised he would go as Soon as his Canoes was made at
9 O Clock the Canoes Came up with us & we Sleept a
little above the Bres[122] –

[p. 8]   Saturday 13 Northerly wind & Cold weather all day at
5 O Clock we left our Camp & in the evening we
Campt 1½ leags above the Sallin[123] hard frost in the
Evening –

Sunday 14 Northerly wind & hard frost in the morn-
ings but fine weather towards midday at 5 O Clock
we Campt at the Enterance of the little River[124] –

Monday 15 Hard frost in the morning but fin [fine]
weather all day, at 2 O clock we Campt [camped]
about two leags Below the Rivier au Pain Binna[125] –

Tusday 16 fine weather all day we Campt at 5 Oclock
about 3 leags above the Rivier au Pain Binna in the
Night it Rained –

Wensday 17 Wasterly wind & Cloudy weather in
the afternoon it Rained we Campt at 3 Ocklock
Ceasar killed a Buffalo which was Separated Between
the Canoes –

Thursday Wasterly wind & Cloudy weather at
3 Oclock we Campt at the foot of the Rapid[126] in the
afternoon it blew hard & Rained

Fraiday 19 Northerly wind & Cloudy weather & Cold
we Came up the 3 Cascads[127] 3 of the Cano [canoes]
was torn a little & 3 packs weat [wet] in my Canoe

at 11 Oclock it Began to Rain & we Campt at the Portage[128] –

[p. 8d]   Saturday 20 Northwast wind & Cold with Rain in the morning But fine weather all day we Came up the Rapids where we Sleepd last night & my Canoe came to the uper end of the Portage de pain[129] where we Dryed our packs the other Canoes Camped at 12 Oclock about 1 leag Below –

Sunday 21 hard frost in the morning at 7 Oclock the other Canoes Came up with us & at 2 Oclock we Campt about 4 leags Below the portage la loch[130] in the afternoon it Rained a little Martain killed one large & 2 little Bears & Ceasar killed a Biech[131] which was Separated between the Canoes –

Munday 22 Sutherly wind & fine weather in the morning at 12 Ockock [sic] we arrived at the Portage[132] in the afternoon Thundered & Rained a little –

Tuesday 23 in the morning the people began to Carrey therir [their] Bagage & they Sleept on the top of the hill[133] I left two of the Canoes at this end of the portage By order of Mr Pond[134] –

Wensday 24 in the morning I went to the other end of the Portage to See if the lack[135] was Clear but I found it Still Covered with Ice our people Slept at the little lack[136] –

[p. 9]   Thursday 25 St Germain Derry Jolleybois & I Came to the end of the Portage to fish our people Slept at the Bon Dieu de Jos Gray[137] –

Fraiday 26 we Sent some fish to the people in the Portage they Sleept a little Beyond the Grand Maskege[138] –

Saturday 27 our people Slept a little this Side of the Grand Maskege – the Ice Disapeared

Sunday 28 at 10 O Clock they arrived at this end of the portage I was obliged to Engage 8 men to go for the two Canoes left at the other end of the portage at 100 ††[139] a man –

Munday 29 at 8 o clock they arrived with the two Canoes & immeadeatly set about gumming them at 11 we left the Portage & Sleept in the Rivier la loch[140] –

Tuesday 30 at 11 O Clock we arrived at the Bottom of the Rivier la loch it Blew so hard we Could not attempt the lack De Bufe[141] till a little before sun Set when we embarked & we Sleept this side of the Grand Bay[142]

Wensday 31 we left our Camp before day & at half past 2 O clock it Blew so hard we was obliged to Camp about half way Between the little Detroit[143] & the Enterance of the Rivier Coruese.[144]

THE
ACCOUNT
BOOK

The Men's Accounts are printed here exactly as they appear, except that the two halves of each account, giving amounts due to the company (usually labelled "Dr") and those due to the man from the company (labelled "Contra"), appear in the original on opposite pages, and here the two halves are printed one above the other. The accounts are all in the same hand except for a few additions which are printed in sans-serif here. General features of the accounts are discussed in the introduction, and each man is listed in the biographies in appendix B. No extensive commentary has been attempted on the inventories of trade goods, but unusual items are dealt with in notes.

pages 13d-14

Dr   Jean Bapt Le Tandre [Letendre]   devant

1785

July 29	To Balance due from last year	670	10
	To Sundries at Fort L. La Pluis p Blotter	368	
	To Sundries on the road p ditto	60	10

1786

June 13	To amt of your acct with Mr Baldwin	92	
	Lvs	1191	
	To Balance due by you	391	

Contra

1786

June 13	By one years Wages	800	
	By Balance due by you	391	
	Lvs	1191	

pages 13d-14

D^r	Antoine Bourcie [Bourcier] dit Lavigne	Millieu	
1785			
July 29	To Balance due from last year	382	3
	To Sundries at Lac la Pluis p Blotter	138	
Augt 25	To Sundries on the way p ditto	26	
1786			
May 31	To Sundries p Isle a la Crosse Book	38	
	To Pierre de Raimond for 2 Skins	24	
		608	
	To Balance due by you	68	3
Contra			
1785			
Oct 13	By Joseph Papan for a capot	40	
1786			
May 31	By one years Wages	500	
	By Balance due by you	68	3
	Lvs	608	3

pages 14d-15
D^r   Pierre Preux   Millieu
1785

July 29	To Balance from last year	267
	To Sundries at Lac la Pluie p Blotter	194
Augt 26	To Sundries on the Way p do	55 10
	To Sundries p Isle a la Crosse Book	136
		Lvs 652 10

1786
June 1   To Balance due by you   152 10
Contra
1786
June 1   By One years Wages   500
          By Balance due by you   152 10

                                              Lvs 652 10

pages 14d-15

D^r   Jean B^t Languedocque   Millieu

1785

July 29	To Balance from last years Book	183
Augt 6	To Sundries pr Blotter at I, la Pluis	335
1786		
June 1	To amt of your acct p Arabasca Book	542
	To 1 fathm Tobo & 1 Bryette* Isle a la Crosse	32
	Lvs	1092
	To Balance due by you	592

Contra

1786

June 1	By one years Wages	500
	By Balance due by you	592
		1092

* Tobacco was formed into twisted ropes which were coiled for transport; it was sold by length. A *brayette* was a breech clout.

pages 14d-15

D^r   Henry Caesar   Devant

1785

July 29	To Balance from last years Book	235
Augt 6	To Sundries at Lac La Pluis p Blotter	330
[1786]		
May 31	To amt of your acct p Arab^a Book	835
	To 1½ fathoms Tobo Isle a la Crosse	45
		Lvs 1445
	To Balance due by you	586

Contra

1786

May 31	By so much to your Credit p Arabasca B^k	59
	By One years Wages	800
	By Balance due by you	586
		Lvs 1445

pages 15d-16
Dr   Jean Bt Lefleur [Lafleur]   Millieu
1785

July 20	To Balance from last years Book	422
Augt 6	To Sundries pd J.B. Rappin at L La P	45
1786		
June 1	To Sundries P arabasca Book	300
		Lvs 767
	To Balance due by you	317

Contra
1786

June 1	By so much to your Cr by Arabasca Book	50
	By one years Wages	400
	By Balance due by you	317
		Lvs 767

pages 15d-16
Dr Pierre Duvalle   Devant
1785

July 29	To Sundries at Lac la Pluis p. Blotter	460
	To Sundries paid St Germain	47
	To 1 fath^m Tob^o	8
1786		
June 1	To Amt p Arabasca Book	970
	To 1 fath^m Tob^o & 1 Lge Knife Isle	
	a la Crosse	26
		Lvs 1511
	To Balance due by you	411

Contra
1786

June 1	By so much forgiven him by Mr Pond	
	when Engaged for 3 years	300
	By Balance due by you	411
	By One Years Wages omitted	800
		1511

pages 15d-16

D^r	Joseph Landrie [Landry] dit Cadien	Gouvern^t		

D^r   Joseph Landrie [Landry] dit Cadien   Gouvern^t

1785

July 29	To Balance from last years Book	378 17
Augt 5	To Sundries at Lac la pluis p Blotter	352
1786		
May 31	To amt of your acct p arabasca Book	811
	To 75 Banches Beads & 1 doz Rings	
	F^t la Crosse	28
June 1	To 1½ fath^{ms} Tob^o & 1 large Knife do	36
		Lvs 1605 17
	To Balance due by you	705 17

Contra

1786

June 1	By one years Wages	800
	By allowed him for Carr^g Canoes in the	
	Portage La Loche	100
	By Balance due by you	705 17
		Lvs 1605 17

pages 16d-17

D^r	Pierre Marcille Millieu		

1785

| July 29 | To Balance from last years Book | | 361 |
| | To Sundries at Lac La Pluis p Blotter | | 304 16 |

1786

June 1	To Amt of Sundries p Arabasca Book		281
	To 1 Calumet*	6^{tt}	
	To 1½ fathms Tob^o	30	
	To 1 fire Steel Isle a la Crosse	2	
		—	
			38

		Lvs	984 16
	To Balance due by you		364 16

Contra

1786

June 1	By So much to your Credit p Ar^a Bk	120
	By one years Wages	500
	By Balance due by you	364 16
		Lvs 984 16

* A *calumet* was properly a ceremonial pipe, but only an ordinary clay pipe may be meant.

pages 16d-17

Dr Joseph Nasplette dit Pass-par-tout   [no rank given]

1785

July 29	To Balance from last years Book	250
	To Sundries at Lac la Pluis p Blotter	400
1786		
June 1	To Amt of your acct p Arab^a Book	566
		Lvs 1216

	To Sundries p^r Arab^a Book since his Engage^{mt}	101 10
June 1	To Sundries at Isle a la Crosse	38
	due by you	Lvs 139 10

Contra

1786

Apl 7	By one years Wages	550
	By his Debt given up to him p his Engagement of this date for 3 yrs	666
		1216

pages 17d-18

Dr Louis Fortin   Gouvernaille

1785

July 29	To Balance from last years Book	602	10
	To Sund^{ies} at Lac la Pluis p Blotter	282	
Augt 26	To Sundries on the way	61	
	To Sundries at Isle a la Crosse	177	
		Lvs 1122	10
	To Balance due by you	322	10

Contra

1786

June 1	By one years Wages	800	
	By Balance due by you	322	10
		Lvs 1122	10

pages 17d-18
Dr Jean B^t Leprise [Laprise]   Millieu
1785

July 29	To Balance from last years Book	260	5
Augt 5	To Sundries pr Blotter at L la Pluis	276	
	To Sundries p do Isle a la Crosse	171	
1786			
June 1	To Amt of your acct p Ar. Book	482	
	To 1 fathm Tobo Isle a la Crosse	20	
		Lvs 1209	
	To Balance due by you	560	

Contra
1786

June 1	By one years Wages	500
	By voyage extra to Arabasca*	100
	By so much to your Credit p A. Bk	16
	By Error in Mr Ponds Book	33
	By Balance due by you	560
		Lvs 1209

* For the extra voyage to Arabasca see Introduction, page xxix.

pages 18d-19
D^r   Jean Bapt Lavallé   Gouvern^l
1785

July 29	To Balance from last years Book	517 10
1786		
June 1	To Amt of Sundries p Isle a la Crosse Bk	429
	Lvs	946 10

1786
June 1   To Balance due by you   146 10
Contra
1786

June 1	By one years Wages	800
	By Balance due by you	146 10
		946 10

pages 18d-19
Dr J. Bt. Brunosh   Millieu
1785
July 29	To Balance from last years Book	430	1
1786	To amt of Sund^{ies} p Arabasca Book	325	
June 1	To 1 Breyette Isle a la Crosse	12	
		Lvs 767	1
	To Balance due by you	294	11

Contra
1786	By so much to your Cr p A. Book	22	10
June 1	By one years Wages	450	
	By Balance due by you	294	11
		Lvs 767	1

---

pages 18d-19
Dr Joseph Hans [Ainsse]   Gouvernaille
1785
July 29	To Balance from last years Book	268

N.B. this man did not come back to the
English River but is gone to some
other post or to Montreal

pages 19d-20

Dr   Joseph Preux   Devant

1785

July 29	To Balance from last years Book		222 10
Augt 5	To Sund^ies at Lac la Pluis p Blotter		242
1786	To Sundries p Arabasca Book		153
	To Sundries at Isle a la Crosse viz		
	1½ fath^ms Tobo pd Brunosh	30	
	1 large Knife	6	
	2 Meas^r Powder & Balls	16	
	1 Small Knife	4	
	Paid for making your Packs	10	
			66
	To Mr Cuthbert Grant for a Gun		125
	To So much you allow for passage of		
	your Woman to the Portage*		149
		Lvs	957 10

Contra

1786

June 1	By one years Wages		800
	By so much to your Credit p A. Book		157 10
		Lvs	957 10

* "The Portage" might be Portage la Loche, if Preux's Indian wife was going there to stay with her relatives for the summer, but it might also have been Grand Portage, if Preux was leaving the Indian Country and taking his wife to Canada.

pages 19d-20

Dr	Joseph Guyette d'Y Masca [Yamaska] [no rank given]	
1785		
Augt 6	To Sundries at Lac la Pluis p Blotter	167
1786		
June 1	To Sundries p Isle a la Crosse Book	66
	To so much answd J.B. Rappin for you	80
	To 1 Hatt	20
	To 1 Bryette	12
	To Sundries at Arabasca	53
	To Balance due you	302
		700
	To Amt of Your acct wt Messrs Frobishers not sent to Lac la Pluis last year* [blank]	

Contra		
1786		
June 1	By one years Wages	500
	By voyage to Arabasca in the Winter†	200
		700
	By Balance du you	302

* The "acct wt Messrs Frobisher not sent to Lac la Pluis" will have consisted of whatever charges the man incurred on his way up from Montreal.
† For the "voyage to Arabasca in the Winter," see introduction, page xxix.

pages 20d-21

Dr Francois Le Blan [Leblanc] devant

1785

July 29	To Balance from last years Book	182
Augt 6	To Sund^{ies} at Lac la Pluis p Blotter	347
	To 1 Tobacco Box at do	6
	To Sundries on the road p Blotter	62

1786

May 30	To 2 Meas. Powder & Balls for Isle Crosse	24
	To 1 fath^m Tob^o	20
	To amt of your acct at Lac La Ronge	78
June 1	To Balance due you	81

Lvs 800

*July**	*To Francois Monette*	*80*
	To Balce	*1*
		81

Contra

1786

June 1	By one years Wages	800

Lvs 800

By Balance due you	81
By Balce	*1*

* Italicized entries were added later than the main entries, but in the same hand.

pages 20d-21
D^r   Joseph Papan   Millieu
1785

Augt 7	To Sundries at Lac la Pluis p Blotter		303
	To Sundries p Isle a la Crosse Book		197
1786			
June 1	To ditto do do		70
		Lvs	570
	To Balance due by you		70
1786			
June 1	By one Years Wages		500
	By Balance due by you		70
		Lvs	570

pages 21d-22

D^r	Jos: Forcier Millieu	
1785		
July 29	To Bal^{ce} from last years Book	6
1786		
June 1	To Sundries p Isle a la Crosse Book	615
		Lvs 621
	To Balance due by you	121
Contra		
1786		
June 1	By one Years Wages	500
	By Balance due by you	121
		Lvs 621

pages 21d-22

D^r	Dom^{que} Ledoux Millieu	
1785		
Augt 6	To P. Smalls note to Lefrance*	50
	To Sundries at Lac la Pluis p Blotter	304
1786	To amt of your acct p A. Book	372
June 1	To 1 Cutteaux resort & 1 f^m Tob^o	25
		Lvs 751
	To Balance due by you	70
Contra		
1785		
July 29	By Balance due you from last year	131
1786		
June 1	By one years Wages	550
	By Balance due by you	70
		751

* Lafrance was probably Ledoux's financial agent in Canada, and also Brousseau's (see page 54); drafts on behalf of these men were sent on authority of Patrick Small.

pages 21d-22
Dr   Jean Bapt Antaya   Gouvernl
1785

Augt 6	To P. Smalls note (say dft) for Balce	103	10
	To Sundries at Lac la Pluis p Blotter	237	
1786	To ditto p Isle a la Crosse Bk	99	
June 1	To Balance due your [*sic*]	464	
		Lvs 903	10

Contra
1785

July 29	By Balance due you from last year	103	10
1786			
June 1	By one years Wages	800	
		Lvs 903	10
	By Balance due you	464	

pages 22d-23

D[r]	Jean Marie Bouche [Bouché] Devant	
1785		
July 29	To Bal[ce] due by you from last year	128
Augt 6	To P Smalls dft on the Co[y] for	100
	To Sundries at Lac la Pluis p Blotter	227
1786		
June 1	To ditto p Isle a la Crosse Bk	240
	To Balance of Sund[ies] p Mr Ponds Book	74
	To Balance due you	161
		Lvs 930

Contra		
Octr 1	By Louis Coté	30
29	By Extra voyage to Arabasca	100
1786		
June 1	By one years Wages	800
		Lvs 930
	By Balance due you	161

pages 22d-23

Dr Chas Papan   Millieu

1785

July 29	To Balance from last year	263 10
Augt 6	To Sundries at Lac la Pluis p Blotter	311
1786		
June 1	To Amt of your acct p arabasca Book	454
	To 1 fath^m Tob^o & 1 Small Knife Isle	
	a la Crosse	34
		Lvs 1062 10
	To Balance due by you	112 10

Contra

1786

June 1	By one Years Wages	550
	By a Debt given him up by Mr Pond	
	when Engaged for 3 years	400
	By Balance due by you	112 10
		Lvs 1062 10

pages 23d-24

D^r	Jos. Landrieffe Gouvernaille	
1785		
July 29	To Balance from last years Book	524
Augt 6	To Sund^{ies} at Lac la Pluis p Blotter	274
1786		
June 1	To Sundries p Arabasca Book	488
2	To 1 fath^m Tob^o & 1 Small Knife Isle a la Crosse	24
		Lvs 1310
	To Balance due by you	510
Contra		
June 1	By one years Wages	800
	By Balance due by you	510
		Lvs 1310

pages 23d-24

D^r   Joseph Laverdure   Millieu

1785

July 29	To Balance from last years Book	441
	To Sundries at Lac la Pluis p Blotter	229
1786		
June 1	To amt of your acct p Arabasca Bk	563
	To 1 fath^m Tob° Isle a la Crosse	20

Lvs 1253

	To Balance due by you	703

Contra

1786

June 1	By one years Wages	550
	By Balance due by you	703

Lvs 1253

pages 24d-25
D^r   Pierre Bellanger   Gouvern^l
1785

July 29	To Balance from last years Book	447	10
Augt 6	To Sund^ies at Lac la Pluis p Blotter	250	

1786

June 1	To Balance given by Mr Pond when Engaged for 3 years P Arab^a Book	102	10

Lvs 800

1787*
Jany 12   Paid in Cash 47^tt7^⁓ Goods 50^tt
                              is 97^tt7^⁓

Contra
1786

June 1	By one years Wages	800

Lvs 800

---

* Entries in sans-serif were added later in another hand. The symbols ^tt and ⁓ represent *livres* and *sous*, respectively. There were 20 *sous* to the *livre*, and 12 *livres* were taken as equivalent to £1 Halifax Currency.

pages 24d-25
Dr Alexis Boyé   Millieu
1785
Augt 6   To Sundries Pr Blotter   366
1786
June 1   To Sundries p Isle a la Crosse Book   253
                                                                                    ———
                                                                    Lvs 619
                                                                                    ———

Contra
1786
June 1   By Bal^{ce} from last year   9
              By one years Wages   500
              By 1 Hatt & 1 pair Shoes   35
              By Ignace Lavallé   75
                                                                                    ———
                                                                    Lvs 619
                                                                                    ———

pages 24d-25
D^r   Pierre La Charité   Millieu
1785
Augt 12 To ½" Pork & 1' flour*   9
      16 To 1"   do   & 1"   do   12
1786
June 1   To Sund^ies p Isle a la Crosse Book   100
          To Balance due to you   269
                                                       ————
                                              Lvs   390
                                                       ————

          To amt of your acct wt Messrs Frobisher
          not Sent to Lac la Pluis   [blank]
Contra
1786
June 1   By one years Wages   390
                                                       ————
                                              Lvs   390
                                                       ————
          By Bal^ce due you   269
                                                       ————

---

* Pork and flour were not part of the diet provided to voyageurs beyond
  Grand Portage, but these food items were sometimes purchased by new
  men, who evidently took some time to get used to the monotonous diet of
  the northwest. The term *mangeurs de lard* was sometimes used to refer to
  those voyageurs who paddled canoes as far as Grand Portage or Lac La
  Pluie but did not winter in the Indian Country.

pages 25d-26

Dr   Joseph Perott [Perrault]   Millieu

1785

July 29	To Balance from last years Book	346	16
Augt 6	To Sundries at Lac la Pluis p Blotter	336	5
1786			
June 1	To amt of your acct p Arabasca Book	439	
	To 1 fathm Tobo Isle a la Crosse	20	
		Lvs 1142	1
	To Balance due by you	490	1

Contra

1786

June 1	By one years Wages	550	
	By so much to your Cr by Araba Book	102	
	By Balance due by you	490	1
		Lvs 1142	1

pages 25d-26

D^r	Louis Brisbois Millieu	
1785		
July 29	To Balance from last years Book	205
1786	To amt of your acct p Arabasca Book	908
June 1	To 1 Calumet & 1 fath^m Tob^o Isle	
	a la Crosse	26
		Lvs 1139
	To Bal^{ce} due by you	689
Contra		
1786		
June 1	By one years Wages	450
	By Balance due by you	689
		Lvs 1139

pages 26d-27

D[r]   Pierre Dumas   Millieu

1785

July 29	To Balance from last years Book	129	10
Augt 6	To Sund[ies] at Lac la Pluis p Blotter	198	
1786	To Amt of your acct p arabasca Book	346	
June 1	To Sundries at Isle a la Crosse	38	
		Lvs 711	10
	To Bal[ce] due by you	211	10

Contra

1786

June 1	By one years Wages	500	
	By Balce due by you	211	10
		Lvs 711	10

pages 26d-27

D^r   Louis Bruisseau [Brousseau]   Millieu

1785

Augt 6	To P. Smalls dft to Lefrance	50
	To Sundries at Lac la Pluis p Blotter	344
1786		
June 1	To amt of your acct p Arabasca Book	395
	To Balance due you	97
		Lvs 886

Contra

1785

July 29	By Balance due you from last years Book	86
1786		
June 1	By one Years Wages	800
		Lvs 886
	By Balance due you	97

pages 26d-27

Dr Janvier Mayotte   [no rank given]

1785

July 29	To Balance from Last years acct	369
	To 1 orignel skin p^d Joly*	10
1786		
June 1	To amt of your acct at Arabasca	728
	Lvs	1107

Contra

1786

June 1	By one years Wages	600
	By 50 Beavers p Arab^a Book	270
	By his Debt p do given him up when	
	Engaged by Mr Pond	237 10
		1107 10

---

* Joly must have been a voyageur present in English River in 1784–5 but not in 1785–6; see his Biography.

pages 27d-28
Dr Jean Marie LEuneau [L'Euneau]   Millieu
1785

July 29	To Balance due by you	181
Augt 6	To Sundries at Lac la Pluis p Blotter	299
	To Sundries on the way p Do	26
1786		
June 13	To amt of your acct wt Mr Baldwin	413
		Lvs 919
	To Balance due by you	419

Contra
1786

June 13	By one years Wages	500
	Balance due by you	419
		Lvs 919

pages 27d-28

D^r   J Bapt. Thesson   Millieu

1785

July 29	To Balance from last years Book	36
1786		
June 1	To amt of your acct p Arab^a Book	465
		Lvs 501

Contra

1786

June 1	By Sundries to your C^r P Arab^a Book	151
	By one years Wages	350
		Lvs 501

pages 27d-28

D[r]   Joseph Morand [Maranda]   Millieu

1785		
July 29	To Balance from last years Book	340
1786		
June 1	To Sundries p Arab[a] Book	766
	Lvs	1106
	To Balance due by you	606
Contra		
1786		
June 1	By one years Wages	500
	By Balance due by you	606
	Lvs	1106

pages 28d-29

Dr Baziel Bodoin   Gouvernaille

1785

July 29	To Balance from last years Book	354
Augt 6	To Sundries at Lac La Pluis p Blotter	433
1786		
June 1	To Amt of your acct p Arab^a Book	358
	To Sundies at Isle a la Crosse	26

Lvs 1171

To Balance due by you   371

Contra

1786

June 1	By One Years Wages	800
	By Balance due by you	371

Lvs 1171

pages 28d-29

D^r	J B^t Gagnier Millieu		

1785			
July 29	To Balance from last year	536	10
Augt 6	To Sund^{ies} at Lac La Pluis p Blotter	216	
1786			
June 13	To Am^t of your acct w^t Baldwin	270	
		Lvs 1022	10
	To Balance due by you	472	10

Contra

1786			
June 1	By one years Wages	550	
	By Balance due by you	472	10
		Lvs 1022	10

pages 29d-30
D^r   Francois Bouché   Millieu
1785

July 29	To Balance from last year	379
Augt 6	To Sundries at Lac la Pluis p Blotter	267
1786		
June 1	To amt p Isle a la Crosse Book	85
	To amt P Arabasca Book	799
	Lvs	1530
	To Balance due by you	680

Contra
1786

June 1	By one years Wages	650
	By voyage to Arabasca & Carr^g Canoes in the Great Portage	200
	By Balance due by you	680
	Lvs	1530

pages 29d-30

Dr   Pierre Aussan   Devant

1785

July 29	To Balance from last year	318	15
Augt 6	To Sundies at Lac la Pluis p Blotter	410	10
1786			
June 1	To Sundies p Isle a la Crosse Book	177	
		906	5
	To Balce due by you	106	5

Contra

1786

June 1	By one years Wages	800	
	By Balance due by you	106	5
		Lvs 906	5

pages 30d-31
Dr Augustin Piccott   [no rank]
1786

June 1	To Sundries at Isle a la Crosse	160
	To Balance due you	438
		Lvs 598
Septr 15	To Cash paid him at Mont^l on acc^t	220^{tt}
Octr 4	To Do paid Mr Corry for him	600
	To Sundries on the Road	56

Contra
1786

June 1	By one years Wages	350
	By Chas Messier answ^d for him	100
	By Ignace Lavalle answ^d for him	140
	By Francois Nadot	8
		Lvs 598
	By Balance due you	438

Entries in sans-serif are in another hand. Mr Corry is presumably Thomas Corry (Wallace, 1934, 434), a retired fur trader who operated as a merchant at L'Assomption, adjacent to Piccott's own parish of Repentigny.

pages 30d-31
Dr   Bapt Guy   Millieu
1785
July 29	To Balance from last year		543
Augt 6	To Sundries at Lac la Pluis p Blotter		269
1786			
June 1	To do p Isle a la Crosse Book		180 10
		Lvs	992 10
	To Balance due by you		492 10

Contra
1786
June 1	By one Years Wages		500
	By Balance due by you		492 10
		Lvs	992 10

pages 31d-32

D^r	Francois Monette Guide		

1785		M.C.	
Augt 6	To P Smalls dft in favor of J Vandriel	600	300
1786			
June	To amt p Isle a la Crosse Book		195
	To Balance due you		734
			1229
1786	To the half 600 M.C^y.* pd. by Messrs Frobisher... the other half being charged last year. tho' not paid then		150
	To Balce due you		664
			Lvs 814

Contra

1785			
July 29	By Balance due you from last year		229
1786			
June 1	By one Years Wages		1000
			Lvs 1229
	By Balance due to you		734
	By Francois Le Blan		80
			814
	By Bal^{ce} due you		664

* "M.C." means "Montreal currency"; a well-established convention was that *livres* earned or spent in the northwest (sometimes called "G.P.C." or "Grand Portage currency") were worth twice those earned or spent in Canada. Entries in sans-serif are in another hand.

pages 31d-32

Dr Joseph Cartier   Devant

1785

July 29	To Balance from last year Book	400
	To Sundries at Lac la Pluis p Blotter	305
1786		
June 1	To Sundries p Isle a la Crosse Book	286
		991

Contra

1786

June 1	By Wages	800
	By [blank] fath^{ms} Bark & Mend^g Canoes	191
		991

pages 32d-33

Dr Paul St Germain   Guide

1785

Augt 6	To Sundries at Lac la Pluis p Blotter	98

1786

June 1	To am^t of your acc^t P Arab^a Book	1382
	To 4 meas. Amunition	16
	To 1 Cartouch Knife	6
	To 1 Buck hand Clasp^g do	5

Lvs 1507

	To Balance due by you	26 10

Contra

1786

July 29	By Balance from last year	22 10
[*sic*]		
June 1	By so much to your Credit p Ar^a Book	458
	By one years Wages	1000
	By Balance due by you	26 10

Lvs 1507

pages 32d-33

D^r   Simon Martin   Devant
1785

July 29	To Balance from last year	34 10
Augt 6	To Sund^ies at lac la Pluis p Blotter	416
1786		
June 1	To Amt of your acct P Araba Book	363
	To Balance due you	23 10
		Lvs 837

Contra
1786

June 1	By Sund^ies P Arab^a Book	37
	By one years Wages	800
		837 10
	By Balance due you	23 10

pages 33d-34

D^r	Joseph Guyette Millieu	
1785		
July 29	To Balance	5
Augt 6	To Sund^{ies} at Lac la Pluis P Blotter	73
1786	To amunition P Arab^a Book	20
June 1	To Bal^{ce} due you	602
		Lvs 700

Contra
1786

June 1	By allowed him for a small keg Rum due him by Mr Pond for help^g to mend Canoes	150
	By one years Wages	550
		Lvs 700
	By Balance due you	602

pages 33d-34
D^r   Francois Le Pin   Millieu
1785
July 29   To Balance due by you   1087
           N.B. this man did not come in to
           the E.R. last year
Contra
           [no entries]

---

pages 33d-34
D^r   Venance   Millieu
1785
Augt 16   to 1″ Pork & 1″ flour   12
          To amt of your acct wt Messrs Frobisher
          not sent to L. la Pluis   781
                                                            ———
                                                            901
                                                            ———

Contra
           [no entries]

pages 34d-35
D^r   Antoine Modeste   Millieu
1786

June 13	To Amt of your acct wt Mr Baldwin	40	
	To Amt of your acct wt Messrs Frobishers		
	not Sent to Lac la Pluis	78	5
		118	5
	To Balance due him	281	15
		400	
Contra			
	By one years Wages	400	
	By Contra Balance due him	281	15

pages 34d-35

Dr   Joachin Cardinal   Gouvern^{lle}

1785		
July 29	To Balance from last year	511 3
Augt 6	To Sund^{ies} at Lac la Pluis p Blotter	316
1786		
June 1	To Sundries p Isle a la Crosse Book	383 10
	Lvs	1210 13
	To Balance due by you	360 13

Contra

1786		
June 1	By one years Wages	800
	By so much omitted for Gum* last year	50
	By Balance due by you	360 13
		1210 13

---

* Gum, collected more likely by Cardinal's wife than by himself, was for mending canoes.

pages 34d-35
Dr Monsr Paul Primeau   [no rank]
1785

Septr 7	To 1 Calimanco Man^t.*	20
	To 1 piece Gart^g	30
	To amt of your acct w^t Mr Baldwin	347
	To Balance due you	112
		Lv 509

Contra
1785

July 29	By Balance from last years Bk	109
	By One years Wages	400
		509
	By Balance due you	112

* A mantle of *calamanco*: "A woollen stuff of Flanders, glossy on the surface, and woven with a satin twill and chequered in the warp, so that the checks are seen on one side only; much used in the 18th c." (*OED*). The next line refers to *gartering*.

pages 35d-36A

D^r	Francois Durrell dit Mactem Millieu		
1785			
July 29	To Balance from last year		682
Augt 6	To Sundries at Lac la Pluis P Blotter		153
1786			
June 1	To amt of your acct P Arabasca Book		224
	To 1½ fathms Tob° & 1 Small		
	Knife I a Cse		34
		Lvs	1093
	To Balance due by you		543
Contra			
1786			
June 1	By one years Wages		550
	By Balance due by you		543
		Lvs	1093

pages 35d-36A

Dr Charles Guyette   Gouvern^{lle}

1785

July 29	To Balance from last year	652	10
Augt 6	To Sundries at L. la Pluis P Blotter	228	
	To Sundries on the way p do	56	
1786			
June 13	To Amt of your acct w^t Mr Baldwin	346	
		Lvs 1282	10
	To Balance due by you	482	10

Contra

1786

June 13	By one Years Wages	800	
	By Balance due by you	482	10
		Lvs 1282	10

pages 36Ad-36B

D^{r}	Francois Jolybois Gouvernaille			
1785				
July 29	To Balance from last years Book			495
Augt 6	To Sundries at L. la Pluis p Blotter			343
1786				
June 1	To amt of your acct P Arab^{a} Book			665
			Lvs	1503
	To Sundries p Arabasca Book			87 10
	To 1 large Knife	6		
	To 1 fire Steel	2		
	To 1 orignel Skin	12		
	To 1½ fathoms Tob^{o}	30		
				50
	due by you		Lvs	137 10
Contra				
1786				
June 1	By one years Wages			800
	By Bal^{ce} given Him up by Mr Pond when engaged for 3 years			703
			Lvs	1503

pages 36Ad-36B

Dr Francois Piché   Devant

1785

July 29	To Balance from last year	519
Augt 6	To Sundries at Lac La Pluis	300
1786	To Sundries p Isle a la Crosse Book	80
June 1	To Sundries P Arabasca Book	716
	Lvs	1615

Contra

1786

June 1	By Sundries p^r arabasca Book	310
	By one years Wages	800
	By so much given him up when engag'd by Mr Pond for 3 years p Book	337
	By so much on acct of a Bellet of 300^{tt} which Mr Pond answd for La: Violette	168
	Lvs	1615

pages 36Bd-37

D^r   Joseph Derry   Gouvernaille

1785

July 29	To Balance from last year	348	5
	To Sund^ies at L. la Pluis p Blotter	457	
1786			
June 1	To amt of your acct P Arabasca B^k	664	
	To 1 Calumet & 1½ fathms Tob^o I^le		
	a La Crosse	36	
	Lvs	1505	5
	To Balance due by you	705	5

Contra

1786

June 1	By One years Wages	800	
	By Balance due by you	705	5
	Lvs	1505	

pages 36Bd-37
Dr Francois La Rivierre [Larivière]   Devant
1785
July 29	To Balance from last year	315
Augt 6	To Sundries at Lac La Pluis	379
1786		
June 1	To amt P Isle a la Crosse Book	140
	To do P Arabasca Book	360
		Lvs 1194
	To Balance due by you	294

Contra
1786
June 1	By one years Wages	800
	By voyage to Arabasca	100
	By Balance due by you	294
		Lvs 1194

pages 37d-38

D^r	Louis Coté Millieu		
1785			
Augt 6	To Sundries at L. la Pluis	174	
1786	To Sundries P Isle a la Crosse Book	183	
J[?]	To J Bapt Rappin for [blank]	150	
	To Balance due you	248	10
		Lvs 755	10

Contra			
1785			
July 29	By Balance from last year	105	10
	By Joseph Derry at L. la Pluis	100	
	By J. Bapt Le Prise	50	
	By one years Wages	500	
		Lvs 755	10
	By Balance due you	248	10

pages 37d-38

Dr Antoine Pagé   Devant

1785

July 29	To Balance due by you from last year	204
Augt 6	To Sund^{ies} at L. La Pluis P Blotter	290
	To Soap at do	6
	To Sundries on the way P do	38

1786

June 1	To Sundries P. Lac la Ronge Book	62
	To Balance due you	200
		Lvs 800

Contra

1786

| June 1 | By one years Wages | 800 |
| | | Lvs 800 |

| | By Balance due you (paid Fainant) | |
| | Grand Portage 3 Augt 1786 – J.F. | 200 |

Words in sans-serif are in another hand; "J.F." is probably for Joseph Frobisher.

pages 38d-39

D^r	Mon^{sr} Taurango [Tourangeau] Commis [nothing]	
Contra		
1785		
July 29	By Balance from last years Book	991
1786		
June 1	By one years Wages 1600 MC.	800
	By Pierre De Raimond answ^d for him	60
		1851

The total is in another hand.

pages 38d-39

D^r   Francois Nadot   Millieu

1786

June 1	To amt of your acct p Isle a Cross Bk	576
		Lvs 576
	To Bal^{ce} due by you	201
	To amt of your acct wt Messrs Frobisher not sent to Lac la Pluies	499 11
		700 11

Contra

1786

June 1	By one years Wages	375
	By Balance due by you	201
		Lvs 576

pages 39d-40

Dr Bonavan Parisien   Devant

1785

July 29	To Balance from last year	569	10
Augt 6	To a Billet to Tranchmontaigne	100	
	To Sund^{ies} at L. La Pluis P. Blotter	342	
1786			
June 1	To amt P Isle a Crosse Book	326	10
		Lvs 1338	
	To Balance due by you	538	

Contra

1786

June 1	By one years Wages	800	
	By Balance due by you	538	
		Lvs 1338	

pages 39d-40

D^r	Joachin Vertifeuil [Vertifeuille] Millieu	
1785		
July 29	To Balance from Last year	140 15
1786		
June 1	To Amt P Isle a La Crosse Book	233
		Lvs 373 15
	To Balance due by you	73 15
Contra		
1786		
June 1	By one years Wages	300
	By Balance due by you	73 15
		Lvs 373 15

pages 40d-41

D^r	Etiene Babeau [Etienne Babeu] Millieu		
1785			
July 29	To Balance from last years Book		250
Augt 6	To Sundries at Lac la Pluis P Blotter		212
1786			
June 1	To Am^t P Isle a la Crosse Book		321 10
		Lvs	783 10
	To Balance due by you		283 10
Contra			
1786			
June 1	By one years Wages		500
	By Balance due by you		283 10
		Lvs	783 10

pages 40d-41

D^r	Simon Reaume Millieu	
1785		
July 29	To Balance from Last years Book	436
Augt 6	To Sund^{ies} at L la Pluis p Blotter	232
1786		
June 1	To am^t P Isle a la Crosse Book	243
		911
	To Balance due by you	411
Contra		
1786		
June 1	By one years Wages	500
	By Bal^{ce} due by you	411
		Livres 911

pages 41d-42

Dr Ignace Lavallé   Gouvernaille
1785

July 29	Balance from last year	10
Augt 6	To P Smalls dft	150
	To Sundries at L. la Pluis P Blotter	287
1786		
June 1	To Augustin Picotte	140
	To Amt P Isle a La Crosse Book	419
	Lvs	1006
	To Balance due by you	46

Contra
1786

June 1	By one years Wages	800
	By Joseph Papan	60
	By voyage to Lac La Ronge	100
	By Balance due by you	46
	Lvs	1006

One the debit side of this account is written, in another hand, a calculation which actually refers to the next account, that of J. Bapt. St Pierre.

pages 41d-42

| D^r | J. Bapt. S^t. Pierre   Millieu | | |

D^r   J. Bapt. S^t. Pierre   Millieu

1786

June 1	To Sundries P Isle a la Crosse Book	165	
	To Balance due you	151	
		Lvs 316	

1787

| Feby 13 | Paid his Mother   46 18 | 23 | 9 |

Contra

1785

| July 29 | By Balance from last year | 16 | |

1786

June 1	By one years Wages	300	
		Lvs 316	
	By Balance due you	151	

On the debit side of the previous account (Ignace Lavallé's) is the calculation $34.18 + 12 = 46.18$, in the hand whose entries are printed in sans-serif here. This evidently was a calculation of the total amount paid to St Pierre's mother, in Montreal currency, which was then halved to give Grand Portage currency, for this account.

pages 42d-43
D^r   Francois Calvé   Millieu
1785
July 29 To Balance from last year   140 18
         N.B. this man Wint^d at Fort des Prairies
Contra
         [nothing]

pages 42d-43

Dr Francois Lefrance [Lafrance]   [no rank]

1785

July 29	To Balance from Last years Book	407	2
		Lvs 407	2
	To Balance	376	2

N.B. this man Died at F^t La Crosse
last Summer...

Contra

1786

Feby 26	By Jos Durrocher for 1 Shirt &		
	1 pr Trous^{rs} ·	21	
	By Fran Nadot for 1 Coliez & Cap	10	
	By Balance	376	2
		407	2

Evidently Durrocher and Nadot bought the dead man's clothes.

pages 43d-44
Dr Chas. Messier   Millieu
1785
July 29   To Balance due by you   103
Augt 6   To P. Smalls dft   100
           To Sund^{ies} at Lac la Pluis P Blotter   128
1786
June 1   To amt p Isle a la Crosse Book   631
                                                          _____
                                                          Lvs 962
                                                          _____

           To Bal^{ce} due by you   362
Contra
1786
June 1   By one years wages   500
           By allowed you for fishing &
           mend^g netts   100
           By Balance due by you   362
                                                          _____
                                                          Lvs 962
                                                          _____

pages 43d-44

Dr Joseph Durrocher   Gov.

1785

July 29	To Balance from last years Book	170
	To Sundries at L. La Pluis P Blotter	471
1786		
June 1	To amt p Isle a la Crosse Book	705
	To amt of Sund^{ies} p L La Ronge Book	80
	Lvs	1426
	To Balance due by you	566

Contra

1785

July 29	By Pierre Jollie	60
1786		
June 1	By one Years Wages	800
	By Balance due by you	566
		1426

pages 44d-45

D^r   J Bapt Rappin [Rapin]   Devant

1785

| July 29 | To Balance due by you | 329 10 |
| Augt 6 | To Sund^{ies} at Lac La Pluis P Blotter | 70 10 |

1786

June 1	To Sundries P Isle a la Crosse Book	80
	To Balance due him	550
	Lvs	1030

| June 1 | To P Smalls Dft on Messrs Frobisher & McTavish for Bal^{ce} when pd 1100 MC. | 550 |

Contra

1786

June 1	By one years Wages	800
	By Louis Cotté	150
	By Jos. Guyette d'ymaska	80
	Lvs	1030
	By Bal^{ce} due you	550

pages 44d-45

Dr Jos: Duchain   Millieu

1785

July 29	To Balance	865
1786	To Amt of your acc^t P A. Book	280 10
	Lvs	1145 10
	To Balance due by you	845

Contra

1786

June 1	By one years Wages	300
	By Balance	845
	Lvs	1145

pages 45d-46

Dr   Phillip Bruilette   Gouverl

1785

July 29	To Balance from last years Book	846
Augt 6	To Sundies pd Rappin at L. La Pluis	100
	To Sundries p. Blotter at do.	186
1786		
June 1	To amt of your Acct p Araba Book	692
		1824
	To Balance due by you	1024
Contra		
June 1	By one years Wages	800
	By Balance due by you	1024
	Lvs	1824

pages 45d-46

Dr Francois Laviolette   Millieu

1785

July 29	To Bal^{ce} from last years Book		547 10
Augt 6	To Sund^{ies} at Lac La Pluis P Blotter		262
1786			
June 1	To Amt of your Acct P Arab^a Book		683
	To Fran. Piché on his acct & in Goods*		300
	To Sundries at Isle a la Crosse		46
		Lvs	1838
	To Balance due by you		888 10

Contra

1786

June 1	By So much to your C^r P Arab^a B^k		400
	By one years Wages		550
	By Balance due by you		888 10
		Lvs	1838

* Only 168^{tt} of Laviolette's payment to Piché was in cash, see Piché's account.

pages 46d-47

D^r	Francois Faniant Gouv^{ll}	
1785		
Augt 6*	To Sund^{ies} at L. La Pluis P Blotter	326
1786		
June 1	To amt of your acct P Araba Book	10
	To Balance due you	497
		Lvs 833

Augt 3	paid this Balance in Acct with his Brother Josh Fainant – J F	

Contra		
1785		
July 29	By Balance from last year	33
1786		
June 1	By one years Wages	800
		Lvs 833
	By Balance due you	497

* The date July 29 was first written, but was crossed out and replaced by
   Augt 6.

pages 46d-47

D^r   J B^{te} Scavoyard   Millieu

1785

July 29	To Balance from last year	347
Augt 6	To Sundries at L La Pluis P Blotter	226
1786		
June 1	To Amt of your acct P Arab^a Book	362
	To 1 fath^m Tob^o & 1 Bryette Isle	
	a la Crosse	32
		967
	To Bal^{ce} due by you	467
Contra		
1786	By one years Wages	500
June 1	By Balance due by you	467
		Lvs 967

pages 47d-48

D^r   Claude Deveau   Millieu

1785

July 29	To Balance from last years Book	160	10
Augt 6	To Sundries at Lac La Pluis P Blotter	129	

1786

June 1	To amt of your Acc^t P Araba Book	591	
	To 1 fath^m Tob^o	20	
		900	
	To Balance due by you	400	

Contra

1786

June 1	By one years Wages	500	
	By Balce due By you	400	
		Lvs 900	

pages 47d-48

D^r   Francois Raimond   Devant

1785

July 29	To Balance from last years Book	288
Augt 6	To Sund^{ies} at L. La Pluis P. Blotter	369
1786		
June	To Amt of your acct P A. Book	462
	To amunition & 1½ fath^m Tob^o Isle	
	a la Cross	50
	To Passage of your Woman	100
		1269
	To Balance due by you	341

Contra

1786

June 1	By so much to your Cr P Araba Bk	28
	By one years Wages	900
	By Balance due by you	341
	Lvs	1269

pages 48d-49
D^r   Mr. J. Baldwin   Clerk
1785

Augt 6	To Sundies at L. La Pluis	50
	To 1 fath^m Strouds	30
1786		
June 13	To Sundries P your own Book	88
	To Balance due you...	450
		618

Contra
1785

July 29	By Balance due him from last year	258
1786		
June	By one years Wages £30 H.Cy.*	360
		618

* Halifax currency.

pages 48d-49
D^r   Alexis Derry   Commis
1786

June 1	To amt of your acct P Arabasca Bk	277
	To Mr Lessieur answ^d for you	175
	To Balance due you	410
		862

Contra
1785

July 29	By Balance due you from last year	262
1786		
June 1	By one years Wages	600
		862
	By Balance due you	410

pages 49d-50
Dr Pierre de Raimond   [no rank given]
1785

July 29	To Balance from last years Book	160
Augt 6	To Sund^{ies} at L. La Pluis P Blotter	111
Sept 12	To Sund^{ies} R. au Rapid	40
1786		
May 31	To Antoine Taurango	60
		Lvs 371
	To Balance due by you	35
Contra		
1786		
May 31	By Jos Cartier for	12
	By Antoine Bourcie for	24
June 1	By One Years Wages	300
	By Balance due by you	35
		Lvs 371

pages 49d-50

D^r   Ambroise La Lond [Lalonde]   Gouvern^{lle}

1785

Augt 6	To Sundries at Lac La Pluis	82
	To Sundries p Isle a la Crosse Book	82
	To Bal^{ce} due you	736
		Lvs 900
	To Amt of your acct at ye Port^{ge} & Mont^l	___
	12 Augt 1786. Settld	
Contra	Septr. 12 To Bazil Ireland 2^{tt}.14⌣ Money	
1786		
June 1	By one years Wages	800
	By voyage to Arab^a	100
		Lvs 900
	By Bal^{ce} due you	736

pages 50d-51
D^r   Monsr Chas Boyé [Boyer]   Commis
1785

July 26	To 1 Small Copper Kettle	20	
	To 1 Boys Shirt	8	
Augt 12	To 1 Indian Bryette	4	10
Sept 18	To 1 Calicoe Shirt	15	
	To 1 Pack Cards	6	
Novr 4	To 4 small Pacquets Beads	16	
	To 1 Calicoe Shirt	15	
	To 1 fathm Strouds	24	

N.B. these articles to be Charg^d at the
Grand Port^{ge}* prices pr agreemt   108 10

Contra
1785
July 29   By Balance from last years acct   1718^{tt} MC^y859
1786
June 1   By one years Wages   2000^{tt}   1000

12th July sent him a State of this Accot J F

* Because Boyer was to be charged Grand Portage prices for goods
  taken at Athabasca, the final pricing had to be done at Grand Portage.

pages 50d-51
Dᴿ   Quisson   Gouvernl
1786
June 1   To amt from Arabᵃ Book   52
          To your acct at Montˡ & the Portge not sent
Contra
1786
June 1   By one years Wages   700
          Settled 11 Augt 1786

pages 51d-52

Dr Chas Doucette   Millieu

1785

Augt 6	To Sundries at Lac La Pluis	132
1786		
June 1	To Amt of your acct P Arab^a Book	767
	To Sundries at Isle a la Crosse	50
		Lvs 949
	To Bal^{ce} due by you	268
	To his acco^t with Messrs Frobishers & Co	73
		341^{tt}

Contra

1786

June 1	By one years Wages	550
	By so much to y^r C^r P Arab^a Book	116
	By Voyage before the Canoes last year	
	at L. La Pluis	15
	By Balance due by you	268
		Lvs 949

pages 51d-52
D^r   Antoine Bleau
1785

| Augt 12 | To 2″ Pork and 2″ flour L La Pluis | 24 |
| | N.B. this man returned from L La Pluis | |

Contra
      [nothing]

---

pages 51d-52
D^r   J. Bapt Bruno   Millau [*sic*]
1785

June 1	To amt of your acct P Isle a La Cross Bk	138	
	To amt of your acct at Mont^l & ye Portge	129	11
		267	11
	To Balance due you	132	9
		400	0

Contra

| | By one years Wages | 400 | |
| | By Contra Balance due him | 132 | 9 |

pages 52d-53

D^r   Nicholas La Liberté   Millieu

1785

Septr 12   To Sundries at L La Pluis &   179
              on the way P Blotter

1786

June 1   To amt of your acct at Lac la Ronge   261
          To 1 fathm Tob°   20
                                                            _____
                                                         Lvs 460
                                                            _____

          To Balance due by you   60
          To am^t of your acc^t at Montreal & y^e Port^{ge}
          at Montreal   137 8
          at Portage   301
          To his Wife 28   14
                          _____
                           452 8

Contra

1786

June 1   By One Years Wages   400
          By Balance due by you   60
                                                            _____
                                                         Lvs 460
                                                            _____

pages 52d-53

D^r   Francois Aubichon [Aubuchon]   Millieu

1785

Augt 27   To amt of Sund^{ies} at L La Pluis & on
          the way   79

1786

June 10   To amt of your acct at L. La Ronge   298
          To Bal^{ce} due you   13
                                                   ―――――――――
                                              Lvs 390
                                                   ―――――――――
          To amt of ye Acct at Mont^l & ye Portge   178 2
                                                        13
                                                   ―――――――――
                                                       165 2

Contra

1786

June 1   By one years Wages   390
                                                   ―――――――――
                                              Lvs 390
          By Bal^{ce} due you   13
                                                   ―――――――――

pages 53d-54

D^r	Nicholas Constantino [Constantineau]	Millieux	
1786			
June 1	To amt of Sundries P Isle a la Crosse Bk	206	10
	To amt of your acct at L. la Ronge	155	
	To ½ fathm Tob°	10	
		Lvs 371	10
	To Bal^{ce} due by you	21	10
	To amt of Your acct at Mont^l ye Port^{ge}	575	16
	due by him	597	6

Contra			
1786			
June 1	By one years Wages	350	
	By Balance due by you	21	10
		371	10

pages 53d-54
Dʳ   Pierre Mayé   [no rank]
1786
June 1   To amt of Sundⁱᵉˢ P Isle a la Cross Bk   157
          To amt of yʳ acct at Montˡ & ye Portᵍᵉ   210

                                                        367
          Due him   8

                                                        375

Contra
          By one years Wages   375

pages 53d-54
Dʳ   Pierre Roy   [no rank]
1786
June 1   To Amt of your acct P Isle a La Crosse   142 10
          To amt of   do   at Montˡ & ye Portᵍᵉ   177

                                                       319 10
          Due him   80 10

                                                       400

Contra
          By one years Wages   400

pages 54d-55
D^r   Amable La Breche   [no rank]
1785

Augt 12	To 1″ flour	6	
16	To ½ fl Rum	12	10
		18	10
	To amt of your acct at Mont^l & ye Portge	131	17
		150	7

1786
Augt 10   To our Note for Balance 479.6   239 13
                                                      390

Contra   [nothing]

pages 55d-56

D^r   Monsr. Toussains Le Sieur [Lesieur]

To my Draft on the Company favor of

Michon	950
To 1 Blanket 2 pts...	60
To 1 do 1 do...	20

1030^{tt} 515

Contra

By Alexis Derry For a Gun	350 175

By 7 Blkts 2½ Pt which Mr Le Sieur
is to take or in their place any
other Goods for their Value – when
he Chuses...   [no price]

This account is entirely in another hand, probably that of Lesieur himself.

[pages 56d-58 are blank]

page 58d
Inventory of Goods left at Arabasca 8th May 1786

4 new Guns
½ Ps H Bay Strouds[1]
1 Capot[2] 3½ Ells
4   do   3
8   do   2½
4   do   1½
1 Chiefs Coat[3]
7 Boys White Shirts
1 Calicoe Shirt
1 Cotton   do
1 Pr Cotton Trousers
2 P Molton Leggins[4]
8 lb Nett Thd [thread]
8½ lb Holland Twine[5]
1 lb Cold Thd [coloured thread]
3 Maitres du Ritz[6]
12 Pr Moyen Sleeves[7]
16   small   do

3 new Kettles
1 Groce [gross] Gun Worms[8]
2   do   Awls[9]
6 lb Beads
2½ Doz: Ivory Combs
  ½ Doz: Horn   do
1   doz: Box[10]   do
4 mill'd Caps[11]
4 large Knives
4 small   do
3 pc Gartering[12]
16 lbs Vermillion[13]
1 Roll Tobacco
1½ Keg Poudre [powder]
3   Bags Ball
1½ do Shot
2 Blkts 3 pts[14]
2   do   2

page 59
Accot of Sundries sent in 2 Canoes to Arabaska the 31st
   May 1786 – to be deliverd Mr Pond by A. Derrie

6 Bales Goods Containing	6 do 2½ do
1½ p^s Blue Strouds	13 do 2 do
1 p^s Scarlet do want^g 5½ yds	3 do 1½ do
2 p^s Red Strouds	3 Cas'd Capots[15]
2½ yds do	1 Cas'd Hatt
3 Blkts 3 pts	1 Chiefs Coat
9 do 2½	30 Doz: large knives
3 do 2	15 doz: small
5 do 1½	1¼ doz: Still [steel] Tobacco
3 do 1	Boxes
1 Capot 4½ Ells	19 lb Vermillion
2 do 4 do	5 doz Box Combs
2 do 3½ do	4 Groce Rings
15 do 3 do	9 Prs large Sleeves
	Continued

page 59d
Accot of Sundries sent to Arabaska: Continued

11 P small Sleeves
1⅔ Groce Awls
7 lb Holland Twine
7 lb Nett Thread
8 Pr Leggins
4 Bunches Beads[16]
6½ Pc Gartering
1 doz: Files
6 doz: fire Steels[17]
4 Razors
6 Worsted Caps
112 Gun flints
9 Japannd Boxes[18]
1 doz: Horn Combs
1 doz: Ivory   do
3 doz: Gun Worms

1 Ps Bed Lace[19]
1 doz: Nons aprittus[20]
10 Maces [masses] B. C Beads[21]
3 Packs playing Cards
10 look^g Glasses
2 Bunches large Brass wire
2   do   Small   do
8 doz: Thimbles
1 Pr Ribbds [ribbands]
7 Maitres du Ritz
1 Skaine Worsted[22]
1 Boys Shirt
½ Doz: Couteaux a
   Cartourche[23]
1 doz Calumets[24]
   Contd

page 60
Accot of Sundries sent to Arabaska, Contd

6 Bales brot forward
1 Case of Irons containing
16 narrow Tranches[25]
12 Broad   do
8 Small Axes
4 half   do
1 large   do
1 Adze
1 Saw
3 half Axes
1 Augur   ⎫
3 small Axes   ⎭ to Derrie[26]

2 Kegs High Wines[27]
3 Kegs poudre
5 Bags Ball
½ do Shot
3 Bales Tobacco
6 Guns
2 Netts & the Canoe Agres[28]
_____

– 21½ Ps including the Guns &
    netts[29]

page 60d
Inventory of Goods left at L'Isle a la Crosse in the Hands of
   Mr Le Sieur – 4 June 1786

5½ yds English Strouds
2½ yds Aurora[30]   do
14 yds Red Strouds
8½ yds blue   do
_____
30½
3 Chiefs Coats
1 Cased Capot[31]
4 Capots 3 Ells
3   do   2½
9   do   2
2   do   1½
1   do   1
4 Mens white Shirts
1 Boys   do
2 Cased Hatts

14 p^r small Sleeves
2 p^r Moyen   do
9 Skaines Worsted
16 Rom as Hhdss[32]
4 p^s Gartering
15^{li} large Brass Wire
4^{li} small   do
1 doz: Japan'd Boxes wt
   Glasses[33]
3 Spring Tobaco   do[34]
3 Bunches Beads
8½ Groce Thimbles
[blank] Hawks Bells[35]
7 doz: Gunworms
38 fire Steels
36 Gun flints
   Continued

page 61
Inventory of Goods left at L'Isle a la Crosse con[d] –

1 large Nattataned [?] Coleur[36]
1 small   do   do
1 pr Nons aprituss
7 doz: Box wood Combs
11 Horn Combs
1 doz Ivory Combs
10 doz large Knives
12 doz + 4 small   do
2 Cartouche   do
10 Buck handled knives
19 Doz: Rings
3 P[r] Scizzars
1 doz: Stone Crosses[37]
8[li] Vermillion
½[li] Cotton Wick
1 Groce Awls

12 yds Lace
14 files (7 of which Damaged)
1 Round –
5 p[r] Arm Bands
6 fine plain Dagues[38]
28 maces B Corn Beads[39]
2 Tin Basons
5 Plain Dags[40]
4 Battle Axes
1 Blkt 2½ Points
2   do   2   –
1   do   1   –
5 packs Cards –
1 Stock Lock –
1 Poudre Horn –
   Continued

page 61d
Inventory &ª Continued

10 Maitres du Ritz
13 pʳ Ox hide Shoes[41]
2 Coleurs[42]
12½ˡⁱ Nett Thd
8ˡⁱ Holland Twine
2¼ˡⁱ fine Sewing Thread
2ˡⁱ Colour'd – do –
2 Bunches Sturgeon Twine
2 Brass Casks
2 yds bleu ⎫
4½ Red ⎰ Strouds
2 Guns
2 Rasps
3 flat Tranches
8 half Axes

5 Cassetetes[43]
12 large Axes ⎫
5 Hand Saws ⎪
5 Augurs ⎪
7 Hows [Hoes] ⎬ All in Use
9 Brass Kettles ⎪
10 Netts ⎪
2 old files ⎭
1 Roll Tobacco
½ do   Damaged
10 Gallon Rum (say) H Wines
½ Keg Poudre
½ Sac Shot & Ball

page 62
Inventory of Goods lefts with Mr Primo 1786 at the Rat
River –

1 Keg Poudre
1 Sac Balls
4½ doz: large Knives
5 doz: small do
3 doz: firesteels
1 Boys Shirt
1 Childs do
3^{li} Vermillion
2½^{li} worsted
4½^{li} Thread
½P^s Gartering
9 doz: Awls
2 Doz: Gunworms

1½ doz: Box Combs
4 Horn   Do
4 Steel Tobacco Boxes
1 Jappan'd   do
1 P Scizzars
1 file
11 Narrow Tranches
8 Broad
1 large Ax
3 small do
1 Padlock
1 Stock lock
1 Nett & Maiters[44]

pages 62d, 63 are blank.

page 63d
Accot of Goods sent by Tourengeaux to Trade with the
Indians between L'Isle à la Crosse & the River au Rapid
– May 1786 –

4 fathoms Strouds
1 pr leggins
1 Brayet[45]
2   do   Garnish'd[46]
2 Pr Large Sleeves
1 pr Moyen   do
2 pr Small
2 doz: large Knives
2 doz: Awls
1 doz Gun Flints
1 Bunch Beads
1 Doz: small Knives

6 Doz: Rings
$1\frac{1}{2}^{li}$ Vermillion
10 firesteels
1 Capot 1½ Ells
1   do   2   do
1   do   3   do
2 Tobacco Boxes
½ Doz. Box Combs
1 P^s Gartering   *
2 look'g Glasses
$\frac{1}{4}^{li}$ Colour'd Thrd
1 flagg

page 64
Accot of Goods found at the Rivierre au Rapid from
Lac la Ronge – 1786 –

½ Doz: large Knives
½ Doz: small   do
3 White Shirts
3 Chiefs Coats
3 Hatts –
2 pollens [?][47]
3 pr Leggins

3 pr Sleeves
2 fathom English Strouds
3 pr leggins
Shot ⎫
Balls ⎬ In a Bag –
Poudre ⎭

pages 64d-71 are blank.

page 71d
Accott of Money Due to the Men & Drafts – Outstanding –[48]

Peltry

602[li]	Joseph Goyette for P. Small df[t] 602	1204 –
paid	Aug[t] Picotte – still Due on his Note	600 –
paid	Francois Monette	1328 –
paid	Francois Fainant	994 –
paid	J.F. Note to Jn° Frille for ⎫ Col. Cambell	310 18
paid	J.F. do to Jos[h] Paul for ⎭	360 –
	J.F. Note to Le Cerfe (Mongran)	653 –
paid	J.F. Note to J. Soullier (Gibeau Wife)	460 –
	do do to Mons[r] Cadott (Blondeau)	1254 15
	do do to Mons[r] Nollin (Bouthilier)	1950
	do do to Mons[r] Barthe	2322 10
Settled	P. Small dft faver Pagé (Fainant)	400 –
do	Jos[h] Fainant – still due him	900 –
	A. Allard to be p[d] Mad[m] Roy	300
	Francois Amiott for his Child	300
	Charles Boyer to be p[d] to his Uncle	2000 –
paid	John Adams – Wages due him	300
	To be paid to Mr Howard for	
	La Deboche 100pd	

	pd Chaurette 452
	pd Bissonette 2626 10
	pd La Verdure 300
	pd L'Ecuyier 130

3603 10paid

19240 13

Balance due Faniant   2094 18

---

page 72 is blank

Pages 72d-73 contain an Index of the names of the men in the English
River Account Book – not printed here. Page 73 is the inside back cover of
the book.

APPENDIXES

APPENDIX A

Indian Names Found in the

English River Book

THE BIG CHIEF, a Chipewyan, whose visit to the fort is described on 1 April in the Journal. Pond instructed him to trade in future at the new fort to be established on Great Slave Lake, a fact which shows that he came from there or beyond. This man may have been the Big Chief, a principal Indian of Mackenzie River, with whom John Thomson traded for the North West Company in 1800–1 (John Thomson's Rocky Mountain Fort Journal 1800–1, in Masson Collection, McGill University. Cited from HBCA Copy No. 124). The Grand Chefre who was at Wentzel's post on the Mackenzie in the fall of 1806 may be the same man (Wentzel's Grand River journal, copy in PAM, Selkirk Papers, vol. 31, 9308).

THE BIG CHIEF'S SON-IN-LAW, presumably a Chipewyan. He is referred to in the Journal for 10 April, and his visit to the fort is described there on 6–7 May.

THE BOUDAR (from *bouder,* to sulk or pout), a Chipewyan, whose visit to the fort is described in the Journal for 6–7 April.

LE BRAS CASSÉ ("the broken arm"), a Cree, whose visit to the fort, where he was clothed as a chief, is described in the Journal for 18–20 April. The Peccant was one of his companions (ibid.). In the summer of 1800 James McKenzie, the clerk in charge at Fort Chipewyan, went to some trouble to cultivate a Cree called the Bras Cassé, so that he or a member of his band would not agree to act as a guide for an XY Company trader who had just reached Athabasca (Masson, 1960, II:392). This is probably the same man. Later in his journal, McKenzie gives a paraphrase of a speech in which the Bras Cassé chided the Montagners for always threatening to kill the Crees, but never acting; in the end the two tribes sat down to drink together (ibid., 398–9). Peter Fidler bought a canoe from the Bras Cassé at Nottingham House, Lake Athabasca, in the spring of 1804 (HBCA B.39/a/5ᵇ, 24, 17 May 1804). In the summer of 1822 "Old Bras Casse's Son" was a North West Company customer in the Fort Chipewyan region (HBCA B.39/a/20, 1, 4 June 1822).

THE CARCAJEAU (*carcajou*, a wolverine), a Cree (Journal 8 April).

THE CHANTAIR (probably *chanteur*, singer), a Chipewyan (Journal, 9 April). An Indian called Chanteur is mentioned in the North West Company's Fort Chipewyan journal for summer 1821, but associated with "Old Bras Casse's Son," a Cree (HBCA B.39/a/20, 1, 4 June 1821), a fact which suggests that this Chanteur was also a Cree.

THE CHIEF CANCRE (*cancre*, a dunce). His association with the Big Chief's Son-in-Law and the Old Chief suggests that he was a Chipewyan (Journal, 10 April). A Peace River Indian called Cancre accompanied Alexander Mackenzie on his second voyage in 1793 as hunter and interpreter (Mackenzie, 1801, 152 and passim), but there is no other reason to identify him with the chief of the English River Book. In June 1821 the North West Company master at Fort Chipewyan sent one of his men "to go up Peace River with the Fool & Band" (HBCA B.39/a/20, 1, 4 June 1821), and The Fool may be The Chief Cancre of the English River Book, or his successor as band leader.

THE ENGLISH CHIEF. This was apparently the most important trading Chipewyan at Athabasca, and his non-arrival in the spring of 1786 was a source of much anxiety (Journal entries of 10, 11, 16–17, 19–20 April). He finally arrived on 21 April, with a total of forty men, the largest single band to arrive during the spring trade, and Pond clothed both the English Chief and the Old Chief (Journal, 21 April). The English Chief was so called, according to Alexander Mackenzie, because he had been a leader of the Chipewyans who took their furs to Churchill Fort. The English Chief accompanied Mackenzie as far as Great Slave Lake in 1789, and appears to have operated as a trading middleman with the Red Knife Indians further north (Mackenzie, 1801, 2, 17). Turnor gives this man's name as Mis-ta-poose (Tyrrell, 1968a, 449 and n), which however sounds like a Cree name. James McKenzie, then a North West Company clerk, traded with members of the English Chief's band at Fort Chipewyan in the spring of 1800 and clothed as a chief one of their number, a man called Marlin (Masson, 1960, II:384). Others in this band in 1800 were called the Old Whitefish and the English Chief's Brother. Although McKenzie's account is not absolutely clear, it seems that Marlin was first recognized as a chief by the traders on this occasion. "He made many ceremonies," McKenzie reported, "before he accepted of the laced coat; he wished to have a red greatcoat, short breeches and cotton stockings, like the English Chief some years ago at the Old Fort; he would not be a petty chief, he aspired to be raised from nothing to the highest pitch of Glory which a Montagner could possibly be raised to" (ibid.). George Simpson traded with an Indian called the English Chief at Fort Wedderburn in 1820–1, and believed that he was the same as the English Chief of Alexander Mackenzie; he may have been a successor as leader of the same band (Rich, 1938, 329). An Indian called "the English Chief's eldest son" traded at Fort Chipewyan in 1822 (HBCA B.39/a/20, 40d, 45). It is possible that the Montagnais (i.e., Chipewyan) Indian named Catherine, daughter of a certain "Chef Anglais", who married François McDonell at Saint-François-Xavier, Red River, on 6 October 1834 (Lareau and Hamelin, 1984, entries 12, 12708), was a daughter of the English Chief. For a recent biography of the English Chief, which accepts that all references are to the same man, see Sloan (1987).

LE GENDRE (the son-in-law), a fort hunter, mentioned in the Journal on 12 and 13 April.

LA GRAIN (presumably *graine*, seed), a fort hunter, mentioned in the Journal on 9 and 17 April. The entries of 16 and 17 April, taken together, show that he was a Cree. James McKenzie traded meat from an Indian called *La Graine* at Fort Chipewyan in July, 1800 (Masson, 1960, II:394), and this may be the same man. Peter Fidler met an Indian whom he calls "the La Grain" at the forks of the Clearwater and the Athabasca in 1805 (HBCA B.39/a/5[b], 54, 28 May 1805).

THE GRAND PICCOTTE (the "tall pock-marked one," from *picoté*, spotted or speckled. *La picotte* is smallpox. Bergeron, 1980, 368). He is mentioned in the Journal on 10 April, as one of the Indians with the English Chief; this suggests that he was a Chipewyan. He may have been a victim of the smallpox epidemic which reached Athabasca in 1782 (see introduction, page xvi).

THE HAND. Two of his band came to the fort on 9 May, and the Athabasca brigade met him and the rest of the band at Pierre à Calumet on the 11th. It was to him that John Ross told his imaginative lie, that the New Concern canoes belonged to the Hudson's Bay Company (Journal, 20 April). Wentzel mentions "the Hand and band" in his Peace River journal of summer 1800 (NA MG19, C1–15, 22), and this may have been the same man as the Indian of the English River Book.

L'HOMME DE CASTOR (the beaver man), a Cree who visited the fort on 3 April (Journal). James McKenzie, in his Fort Chipewyan journal of 1799–1800, refers to an Indian called The Beaver, perhaps the same as L'Homme de Castor, who had forced one of the voyageurs, Pierre Labrie, to return to the fort from his lodge without adequate food or clothing; Labrie's feet were badly frostbitten, and he was brought to the fort on a sledge and soon after died. McKenzie decided to take no steps to punish the Beaver for his callous behaviour, since he was a valued customer (Masson, 1960, II:375, 378–9).

THE OLD BLIND WOMAN (not necessarily a proper name), a member of The Shining Rock's band. She and her son visited the fort on 3 April (Journal).

THE OLD CHIEF, an important trading Chipewyan, who was clothed by Pond, along with the English Chief, when the two arrived at the fort on 21 April (Journal). On 1 April he was on the other side of Lake Athabasca, and sent a young man in for tobacco. On 10 and 21 April it is stated that he "was with Derry this winter," presumably at a temporary outpost commanded by the clerk, Alexis Derry, whose location is unknown (see introduction, page xix).

L'ORIGNAL (orignal, moose), a fort hunter, mentioned in the Journal with La Graine on 9 April.

LE PECCANT (*peccant*, a marten), a Cree, to judge by his association with *Le Bras Cassé* who arrived at the fort on 19 April (Journal).

LE PETIT ORIGNAL (the little moose), a Cree fort hunter, apparently distinct from L'Orignal, mentioned in the Journal on 15 April.

THE SHINING ROCK ("*La Roche qui reluit*"). His band was raising bark for canoes on 3 April when The Old Blind Woman and her son, two of its members, arrived at the fort; the band itself arrived "from above" on 11 April (Journal). James McKenzie records in his Fort Chipewyan journal of 1799–1800 that he traded with a Cree called the Roche-que-reluit's brother, apparently an important customer. This suggests that La Roche qui reluit himself was a Cree. In September 1804, Peter Fidler traded provisions from "the Shining Rocks" and his companions, the leader of whom was referred to as the "New Co Chief," presumably because he had given his hunt to the XY Company in previous years (HBCA B.39/a/5ᵇ, 35d–37).

THE TITTONS (*tétons*, breasts), "Chief of the Beaver Indians," whose visit to the fort is described on 1 and 2 April (Journal). He is probably the same as "Captn Too-toose ... the greatest Warr Chief they have amongst them," whom Philip Turnor met at Fort Chipewyan in 1791 (Tyrrell, 1968a, 453). Earlier, Turnor had give *Too-toos Sack-a-ha-gan* as the Cree name for "the Paps Lake" (ibid., 400). Turnor reported that Too-toose had led a war party to the Arctic Ocean in the summer of 1791, and had killed several Inuit (ibid., 453). Alexander Mackenzie refers to an Indian called The Téton, who was trading with Roderick McKenzie on the north shore of Great Slave Lake in 1790–1 (Lamb, 1970, 444); this may or may not be the same. The Indian called "Big Bubbies" by George Simpson, who traded at Fort Wedderburn on Lake Athabasca in 1820–1, was conceivably the same as The *Tétons*, or his successor as leader of his band (Rich, 1938, passim). Indians called the Grand Teton and the Old Teton both traded at Fort Chipewyan in 1822 (HBCA B.39/a/20, 32 and 39d).

APPENDIX B

Biographies of Voyageurs

and Traders

AINSSE, JOSEPH, *gouvernail*, not in English River 1785–6 (account pages 18d–19). The name (spelled *Hans* in his account) is the same as that of Joseph-Louis Ainsse (1744–1802), interpreter and fur trader (for whom see Armour, 1983a), but the two men cannot be the same, and it seems unlikely that any son of Joseph-Louis would have been old enough to serve as a *gouvernail* by 1784–5.

ANTAYA, JEAN-BAPTISTE, *gouvernail*, Île-à-la-Crosse, wages 800 *livres* (account pages 21d–22). The family Antaya or Pelletier *dit* Antaya was well established at Sorel in the eighteenth century. This man was probably the Jean-Baptiste Antaya, son of Jacques Antaya and Marguerite Abram or Demarait, who was born at Sorel in 1757, and may be the "Btite Antaya" who appears as a canoeman on a trading licence granted to James McGill and Charles Paterson, apparently in 1774, to take five canoes to Grand Portage (University of Saskatchewan Special Collections, Morton Collection, Fur Trade Licences, 314). Another Jean-Baptiste Antaya, born at Sorel in 1746, was probably the man of this name who was engaged by Paul Hubert Lacroix in 1770 to go to Michilimackinac (APQ *Rapport*, 1932–3, 296; this man had settled down at Sorel by 1776, to judge from records of baptism of his children in the Saint-Pierre-de-Sorel register). The Jean-Baptiste Antaya listed in the English River Book must be the English River guide of 1791 whom John McDonald of Garth called "Antyme" (Masson, 1960, II:18). Antaya was guide for part of the English River brigade going out in June 1793 (NA MG19, C1–5, 48). He seems to have retired from English River a few years later, and in 1799, at the age of forty-two, he married his twenty-three-year-old cousin, Catherine Antaya, at Sorel. Antaya soon after began a career as a Grand Portage guide, taking brigades of the large Montreal canoes between that city and Grand Portage or (after 1803) Fort

William. He is mentioned in this capacity in 1804 (Gates, 1965, 198) and 1816 (PAM, Selkirk Papers, vol. 31, 9221–4; this is an apparently complete list of North West Company canoemen between Montreal and Fort William, evidently seized by Lord Selkirk in 1816). These duties, though important, did not require Antaya to winter in the Indian Country, and he and Catherine Antaya had seven children, baptized at Sorel between 1802 and 1820. Jean-Baptiste Antaya died on 9 January 1821 and was buried at Saint-Pierre-de-Sorel two days later; his widow survived until 1843. (The family details are all from the registers of Saint-Pierre-de-Sorel, summary copy in ANQ-M.)

AUBUCHON, FRANÇOIS, *milieu*, Lac La Ronge, a new man in 1785, wages 390 *livres* (account pages 52d–53). This surname, variously spelled, is found at Sorel in the eighteenth century. Aubuchon's wages are those of an inexperienced man, and so he was probably not the François Obuchon who was engaged by Dejordy de Villebon on 30 December 1758, to go to Grand Portage (APQ *Rapport*, 1932–3, 254). The François Obishon who was in Athabasca for the North West Company from before 1811, and was paid off in 1813 (HBCA F.4/32, 762), could be this man.

AUSSAN, PIERRE, *devant*, Île-à-la-Crosse, wages 800 *livres* (account pages 29d–30). This is also a well-established Sorel family. A Pierre Ossant was baptized at Saint-Pierre-de-Sorel in 1742, and a Pierre Hossan in 1753 (Saint-Pierre-de-Sorel parish register, copy at ANQ-M).

BABEU, ÉTIENNE, *milieu*, Île-à-la-Crosse, wages 500 *livres* (account pages 40d–41). This man may be the Etne. Babut who is listed on a trade licence granted to Benjamin and Joseph Frobisher in 1772 to take three canoes to Grand Portage (Morton Collection, Fur Trade Licences, 223), and he could also be Étienne Barbu, a voyageur in English River in 1804 (Masson, 1960, 1:400), and the Étienne Babeu who is listed in the North West Company's great ledger of men's accounts for 1811 to 1821, also assigned to English River (HBCA F.4/32, 53). This last Étienne Babeu was taken over by the Hudson's Bay Company and retired to Canada in 1822 (HBCA B.239/g/1, 33). If all of these references are to the same individual, they represent a fur trade career of at least fifty years.

BALDWIN, J., clerk, wages £30 Halifax currency or 360 *livres* (account pages 48d–49). The references to "Mr. Baldwin's Book" in some men's accounts show that Baldwin was in charge of a post somewhere in English River in 1785–6. Its location is not given, but it may be established from a journal kept by Malchom Ross, a Hudson's Bay Company servant, during a trip from Churchill to Cumberland House in the late summer of 1786. Ross met Baldwin en route to his wintering ground on 12 September 1786; Ross gives Baldwin's Christian name as Jurial (HBCA B.49/a/18). Elsewhere in the same journal, Ross noted that "Primo" – mistaken by Ross for Louis Primot, a sometime Hudson's Bay Company employee, but now recognizable as Baldwin's associate in the English River Book, Paul Primeau – and another man had remained for the summer on the Churchill near the present Pukatawagan; that the Canadians had wintered in 1785–6 on what is now called Kississing Lake (this, then, was where Baldwin's post was); and that they had been sending one or two canoes into the Rat River country for three years (HBCA B.49/a/18, entries of 6, 8 and 14 September 1786; and comments on Ross's route in 1786, in Tyrrell, 1968a, 598, and Morton, 1973, 441). Baldwin had left Rat River, and perhaps the northwest, by 1789–90, when Robert Thomson was in charge of the district. William McGillivray's English River journal of that season remarks about Rat River: "Our intelligence as to the number of Indians in that quarter, has always been false We were made to believe by Baldwin & all that pretended to know the Country that there were 50 à 60 Indians – instead of which their are only 10 men belonging to the place" (NA MG19, C1–4, 7).

BELLANGER, PIERRE, *gouvernail*, Athabasca, wages 800 *livres* (account pages 24d–25). He was engaged by Pond on 9 April 1786 for three years, "the first to stay in the Countery, & the other two to go to the Portage" (Journal). He probably helped establish the new posts from Athabasca in the summer of 1786. There was a Pierre Bélanger working for the North West Company in the Nipigon district in 1805 and 1811 (Masson, 1960, 1:408; HBCA F.4/32, 109), but there is no reason to think that this was the same man.

BLEAU, ANTOINE (account pages 51d–52). Placed on the English River books in 1785, he apparently did not go beyond Lac La Pluie.

BODOIN, BAZIEL, *gouvernail*, Athabasca, wages 800 *livres* (account pages 28d–29). Not mentioned in the Journal. Bazil Beaudoin was engaged by François Winter (probably acting for the Frobishers and the North West Company) on 14 May 1783, to go to Grand Portage (APQ *Rapport*, 1946–7, 322). A Bazil Beaudoin was a North West Company employee at Michipicoten and The Pic, Lake Superior, in 1811–14 if not before (HBCA F.4/32, 120).

BOUCHÉ, FRANÇOIS, *milieu*, Athabasca, wages 650 *livres* (account pages 29d–30). He is mentioned in the Journal on 8 and 23 April. The name is very common among voyageurs (see APQ *Rapport*, 1932–3, 251, 279, 301; Masson, 1960, 1:396, 400; and HBCA F.4/32, 47, 56, 89, 133, 136, 1049). Two or three of these individuals may have been the same as the François Bouché of the English River Book, but identifications are uncertain. The well-known Métis, Jean-Baptiste Bouché, also know as Waccan, a stalwart of the North West Company and later the Hudson's Bay Company in north-central British Columbia (Morice, 1905, 252–7), was already assisting in the region in 1806 (Lamb, 1960, 237), and therefore was probably born no later than the late 1780s; either François or Jean-Marie Bouché may have been his father. Waccan's mother, whose name and tribe are unknown, later seems to have married Duncan Livingstone, the clerk who first opened up Mackenzie River to trade and was killed in 1799 (Masson, 1960, 1:95), since the interpreter Duncan Livingstone, presumably this clerk's son, was Waccan's half-brother (Morice, 1905, 254–5).

BOUCHÉ, JEAN-MARIE, *devant*, Athabasca, wages 800 *livres* (account pages 22d–23; see also Louis Coté's account, pages 37d–38). He is mentioned in the Journal on 25 April and 8 May; the entry for 8 May shows that "Bouché's canoe" was one of the eight that went out from Athabasca in May 1786, and since most of the other canoes are named for their *devants*, this one must have been Jean-Marie's. The payment to him on 29 October 1785 of 100 *livres* for an "Extra voyage to Arabasca" may be evidence for a reinforcing expedition from Île-à-la-Crosse to Pond's fort, late in the fall of 1785, in response to the appearance of John Ross and the New Concern in Athabasca. The deposition of John McDougald in the Selkirk Papers (vol. 60, 15799) mentions a Jean-Marie Boucher, a half-breed, whose sister was the "woman" of John Thomson, the North West Company partner at English River. John Thomson's will, dated 1824, left his estate to his wife Françoise Boucher and their six children (HBCA A.44/2, 66). It seems likely that the younger Jean-Marie and his sister Françoise were Métis children of Jean-Marie of the English River Book. Dr Mary Black-Rogers has traced the younger Jean-Marie as a North West Company employee at Athabasca (1812–14) and English River (1815–21); he retired to Canada in 1822, leaving a family at Île-à-la-Crosse. He is not to be confused with another Jean-Marie Boucher, from Berthier, born about 1801, who hired with the North West Company in 1820 (HBCA F.4/32, 58) and can be traced in Peace River, and later Churchill and York Factory, retiring to Red River in 1836 (Rich, 1955, 215–18). A petty trader named J.M. Bouché who had set up to trade with voyageurs on the Kaministiquia canoe route in the summer of 1803 (Coues, 1965, 219) may have been the same as the Jean-Marie Bouché of the English River Book.

BOURCIER (*dit* LAVIGNE), ANTOINE, *milieu*, Île-à-la-Crosse, wages 500 *livres* (account pages 13d–14; see also Pierre de Raimond's account, 49d–50, and that of Joseph Papan, 20d–21). The family Boursier *dit* Lavigne was found at Châteauguay, Lachine, and Laprairie in the eighteenth century (Tanguay, 1871–90, II:430). Antoine Bourier [*sic*] *dit* Lavigne was one of "nine men equipt (on their own account) for the Missouri" who left the North West Company's Fort Espérance, Qu'Appelle River, in December 1793 (Masson, 1960, I:286). One Antoine Bourcier was a voyageur at La Pointe, Lake Superior, in 1804 (ibid., 411).

BOYÉ, ALEXIS, *milieu*, Île-à-la-Crosse, wages 500 *livres* (account pages 24d–25). No further information.

BOYER, CHARLES, clerk or *commis*, Athabasca, wages 1000 *livres* Grand Portage currency (account pages 50d–51). There were two fur traders of this name, who were combined into one figure in the only extensive account of the subject, that of A.S. Morton (1937, 87–100). The man in the English River Book is called "Charles Boyer, Junr," in a list of debts recorded at the time of the formation of the new firm of McTavish, Frobisher & Co. in 1787 (Wallace,

1934, 80–1), and he may be the Charles, son of Charles Boyer and Jeanne Supernant, who was baptized at Laprairie in 1744 (Tanguay, 1871–90, II:446). An older Charles Boyer, perhaps this man's father, was a partner of fur traders Forrest Oakes and Peter Pangman in the 1760s and 1770s (Morton, 1937), and other members of the family may be the "Francis and Mishel Buoy" who were reported to be in charge at Lac La Pluie in 1771 or earlier (Wallace, 1934, 41). Michel Boyer, *negociant*, and Charles Boyer, voyageur, appear in the Michilimackinac register in the early 1760s, and Michel's son Charles was born and baptized at Michilimackinac in 1761 (Faribault-Beaurégard, 1982, 122–3, 132, 135–7, 145, 166, 168). The younger Charles Boyer is probably the man who was helping to build a post on the Assiniboine River for John Ross in 1781, when it was attacked by Indians (Morton, 1937). By 1784–5 Boyer was in Athabasca (see page 185, note 103), and he is frequently mentioned in the English River Book Journal of the next season as a trader and canoe builder. The Journal shows that he was to take an expedition to Peace River in the summer of 1786. Boyer remained on Peace River after the coalition of 1787 but left Athabasca in the spring of 1789, anxious to settle his account at Grand Portage (Lamb, 1970, 429, 431, 433, 436, 438). Boyer probably did not go back to Athabasca but in 1793–5 he was in charge of the North West Company's post at Lac La Pluie in northwest Ontario, where John McKay, the Hudson's Bay Company servant opposing him, found him a courteous neighbour, an excellent trader, and a skilful canoe builder (HBCA B.105/a/1 and 2, passim). Boyer was not at Lac La Pluie in 1795–6, and he must be the Charles Boyer who engaged at Montreal as a *commis* with the North West Company for three years, on 4 March 1796, but was released from this engagement eleven days later (ANQ-M, CN1–29 (Étude Beek), documents 1030, 1038). There is no indication that he returned to the Indian Country again.

BRISBOIS, LOUIS, *milieu*, Athabasca, wages 450 *livres* (account pages 25d–26). Engaged on 7 April 1786 to winter three years at Great Slave Lake; also mentioned in the Journal on 23 April. He may be the Louis Brisebois who was baptized at Sainte-Geneviève-de-Montréal in 1754 (Tanguay, 1871–90, II:472), and the Louis Brisbois who is listed as a canoeman on a trade licence granted in 1769 to Basile Irelande, on behalf of Dobie and Frobisher, to take two canoes to

Michilimackinac (Morton Collection, Fur Trade Licences, 61). A voyageur of this name was working for the Hudson's Bay Company in 1821–2 at Île-à-la-Crosse, and retired to Canada in 1822 (HBCA B.239/g/1, 33).

BROUSSEAU, LOUIS, *milieu*, Athabasca, wages 800 *livres* (account pages 26d–27). Mentioned in the Journal on 3 and 13 April 1786. He is probably the Brousseault who was to assist Mr Wentzel at Grand Marais, Peace River, in the summer of 1800 (Masson, 1960, II:391–2; and Wentzel's journal fragment of this season, NA MG19, C1–15). Louis Brousseau was an interpreter at Athabasca in 1806 (Wallace, 1934, 219), and was still in that district in 1811–14 (HBCA F.4/32, 22), going to Montreal in 1814. The Louis Brusseau who came up to English River in 1815, and served the North West Company in that district till 1820, was probably the same man, for although his account in the company ledger is separate, his wages – the rather high figure of 700 *livres* – are the same in both accounts (HBCA F.4/32, 145). Louis Brousseau probably left descendents in the northwest, for Wentzel refers in 1800 to "Brousseault's family," and "Brousseault's sons" who were then old enough to perform casual duties for the North West Company (NA MG19, C1–15, 23, 25). Simon Brousseau, who worked briefly for the North West Company at English River but died in 1819 or 1820, was certainly a son of the Louis Brusseau who was at English River at the same time (HBCA F.4/32, 125, 145).

BRUILLETTE, PHILIPPE, *gouvernail*, Athabasca, wages 800 *livres* (account pages 45d–46). Mentioned in the journal on 15 and 24 April 1786. No further information.

BRUNO, JEAN-BAPTISTE, *milieu*, Île-à-la-Crosse, wages 400 *livres* (account pages 51d–52). A new man in 1785. One Baptiste Bruno was a clerk or interpreter at Upper Fort des Prairies, Saskatchewan River, in 1799 (Masson, 1960, I:63). A Jean-Baptiste Bruneau was one of the North West Company voyageurs who accompanied David Thompson into the mountains in 1810 (Coues, 1967, 928).

BRUNOSH, JEAN-BAPTISTE, *milieu*, Athabasca, wages 450 *livres* (account pages 18d–19; see also Joseph Preux's account, 19d–20).

Mentioned in the Journal, 24 April and 6 May 1786. Brunosh was an interpreter at Athabasca in 1806 (Wallace, 1934, 219) but is not in the North West Company's great ledger, HBCA F.4/32, which starts in 1811; he presumably had retired or died by that date.

CAESAR, HENRY, *devant*, Athabasca, wages 800 *livres* (account pages 14d–15). He was engaged on 12 April 1786 to winter three years at Peace River, and his canoe set off for Lac La Pluie on 8 May. Also mentioned in the Journal on 9 and 23 April and 21 May.

CALVÉ, FRANÇOIS, *milieu* (account pages 42d–43). In English River 1784–5, and so carried over on the books, but at Fort des Prairies (Saskatchewan River) in 1785–6.

CARDINAL, JOACHIM, *gouvernail*, Île-à-la-Crosse, wages 800 *livres* (account pages 34d–35). He is probably the Cardinal mentioned by Mackenzie as in English River in 1787 (Lamb, 1970, 426). Joachim Cardinal was an interpreter in Athabasca in 1806 (Wallace, 1934, 218), and was still in Athabasca in 1811–12, apparently retiring from the North West Company at the end of that season (HBCA F.4/32, 153). His "adopted and natural daughter," Jane Cardinalle, was the country wife of Thomas McMurray, the North West Company partner, and is named in McMurray's will of 1824 as the mother of his six "adopted and natural children" (HBCA A.36/10, 116–17).

CARTIER, JOSEPH, *devant*, Île-à-la-Crosse, wages 800 *livres* (account pages 31d–32; see also Pierre de Raimond's account, pages 49d–50). This man had one of the longest fur trade careers on record. According to the Hudson's Bay Company's Northern Department servants' accounts for 1824, Cartier was then aged 72, a native of Sorel, and had fifty-seven years of service with the company and its antecedents (HBCA B.239/g/4, 37). This information would place his birth about 1752, and his entry into the fur trade about 1767. He was probably a member of the Cartier family who lived at Saint-François-du-Lac, and perhaps the Joseph Cartier who was baptized at Sorel in 1756 (Tanguay, 1871–90, II:571). He probably was a voyageur in his teens, but the first definite reference to him is in the English River Book, when he was already a *devant* and canoe mender. In the fall of 1786 Alexander Mackenzie, who had spent the previous season trading for the New Concern in English River, advised his cousin Roderick McKenzie, his replacement in that district: "Take care of Mr. Cartier, Mr. McGillivrays interpreter as he is a very keen insinuating fellow. Keep every thing as secret as you can from your men, otherwise these old voyageurs will fish all they know out of your Green Hands" (Lamb, 1970, 424). Cartier, whose name William McGillivray spelled "Quartier," appears prominently in McGillivray's Île-à-la-Crosse journal of 1793, trading with Indians, getting bark for canoes, and helping to guide the outward brigade in the spring (NA MG19, C1–5). David Thompson noted "Monsr" Cartier at Cumberland House in June 1797 (Coues, 1965, 629). The "Quartin" who was sent by Donald McTavish from Lac Verd (Green Lake), English River, with three canoes to build a house at Lac La Biche in the fall of 1798 (Lamb, 1970, 476), is probably a transcription error for "Quartier" or Cartier, since David Thompson, who took over the Lac la Biche post that winter, mentions a Joseph as well as a François "Quartier" among his men (Coues, 1965, 1001). Joseph Cartier is listed in the establishment of Upper English River in 1799, wages 1000 *livres* (Masson, 1960, 1:62). In 1804–5 David Thompson, in charge at Cumberland House, assigned Cartier to the North West Company's winter outpost on Cranberry Lake, and the following summer Cartier and one Morren were sent to Kaministiquia (Fort William), probably to return to Canada (Coues, 1965, 626–30). The "Caste" whom Peter Fidler encountered at Grand Rapids on 24 June 1805, acting as the guide for three North West Company canoes from the Rat River district, may have been Cartier (HBCA B.39/a/5b, 55d). Cartier seems to have spent the winter of 1805–6 at Sorel, where his daughters Louise and Charlotte were baptized on 12 October 1805; no mention is made of their mother in the baptismal entry, and she was probably an Indian or Métis who had remained in the Upper Country (Saint-Pierre-de-Sorel parish register, copy in ANQ-M). Cartier went back to the northwest for the next season and is listed as a guide for English River in 1806 (Wallace, 1934, 219). He was still in English River in 1811–12, was paid off in 1812, but rehired for the Columbia Department in 1813 (HBCA F.4/32, 182). He was with Alexander Henry the younger at Fort George, Columbia River, in 1813–14 (Coues, 1965, 785–6, 840, 868, 890–2, 900, 905, 910). Cartier was taken over by the Hudson's Bay Company at the union of the two companies in 1821 (HBCA B.239/g/1, 39) and remained in the Columbia Department. He helped with the closing of Fort George in March 1825 (Merk, 1968, 122, the name is spelled "Cartie") and the next fall is noted at Fort Vancouver (Rich, 1941, 11). He finally retired to Canada in 1827, over seventy years of age, with a credit balance on the company's books of £101/5/5 (HBCA B.239/g/6, 43). Although he probably had relatives still at Sorel, he seems not to have retired there, since his burial does not appear in the register of Saint-Pierre-de-Sorel.

CONSTANTINEAU, NICHOLAS, *milieu*, Lac La Ronge, wages 350 *livres* (account pages 53d–54). A new man in 1785. The "Constantineault" who was in English River in 1786–7, an employee of the New Concern (Lamb, 1970, 424), may have been a different man, or Nicholas may have been induced to join the other side. The Métis voyageur, Jean-Baptiste Constantineau, *dit* "Bob," who was in Athabasca for the North West Company beginning in 1818–19 (HBCA F.4/32, 239), may have been this man's son. The Nicholas Constantin who was at Athabasca from before 1811 till 1821 (HBCA F.4/32, 161), was taken over by the Hudson's Bay Company and retired to Canada in 1822 (HBCA B.239/g/1, 38), may have been the same as this Nicholas Constantino.

COTÉ, LOUIS, *milieu*, Île-à-la-Crosse, wages 500 *livres* (account pages 37d–38; see also J.-M. Bouché's and J.-B. Rapin's accounts, 22d–23 and 44d–45, respectively). He is likely the Louis Coté listed as a canoeman for the Frobishers in 1772 and 1774 (Morton Collection, Fur Trade Licences, 223, 314). He may be the Coté, Christian name unknown, who with Simon Réaume was left in charge of the English River outpost at Lac d'Orignal for the summer of 1793 (NA MG19, C1–5, 34).

DERRY, ALEXIS, *commis*, Athabasca, wages 600 *livres* (account pages 48d–49; see also account of Toussaint Lesieur, 55d–56). His salary suggests a moderately experienced man, but he seems not to be mentioned elswhere in the fur trade literature and must have left the North West Company by about 1790. The Christian name Alexis was in use in the Déry family at Point-du-Lac in the eighteenth century (Tanguay, 1871–90, III:358), and this man was probably a member of that family. The Journal references to "the old Chief that was with Derry" (10 and 21 April) suggest that Derry operated a winter outpost from Athabasca during 1785–6, though by 2 April he was back at the main fort. One of the goods inventories in the English River Book (pages 117ff) shows that Derry accompanied the Athabasca brigade outward in the spring of 1786 until it met a load of goods coming up from Île-à-la-Crosse, and that he then returned with these goods to Athabasca. It had been arranged that he would take an outfit to Great Slave Lake that summer and build a trading house, to which Cuthbert Grant was to come with a full outfit in the fall (Journal, 1 April). This plan probably went forward (see introduction, page xxii).

DERRY, JOSEPH, *gouvernail*, Athabasca, wages 800 *livres* (account pages 36Bd–37; see also Louis Coté's account, pages 37d–38). He may have been one of the voyageurs who was drowned in Slave River in the fall of 1786; see introduction, page xxxvii.

DEVEAU, CLAUDE, *milieu*, Athabasca, wages 500 *livres* (account pages 47d–48). Engaged on 13 April 1786 to winter three years at Peace River, he is also mentioned in the Journal on 3 and 25 April. A Claude-Joseph Devau, who was baptized at Sainte-Anne-de-la-Pérade in 1763 (Tanguay, 1871–90, III:410), may be this man.

DOUCETTE, CHARLES, *milieu*, Athabasca, wages 550 *livres* (account pages 51d–52). He is called Charles *Cadien* in the Journal entry, on 3 April 1786, recording his engagement to winter three years at Great Slave Lake. He had not been in the Upper Country in 1784–5, but his wages, 550 *livres*, suggest that he was an experienced canoeman, as does the fact that he was employed in 1785 for a special "Voyage before the Canoes last year at L. La Pluis." *Cadien* must be for *acadien* (I am indebted to François Lafortune for this suggestion), and Doucet is an Acadian name. The other Cadien at Athabasca in 1786 was Joseph Landry; Landry is also an Acadian name, and there were frequent marriages between the Doucets and the Landrys (Tanguay, 1871–90, III:438–9, and v:127–31). A Charles Doucet, son of Charles Doucet and Marguerite Landry, was baptized at Saint-Pierre-de-Sorel on 19 January 1766, and it is likely that the two Cadiens at Athabasca were relatives. They both accompanied Alexander Mackenzie to the Arctic Ocean in 1789 and to the Pacific in 1793 (Mackenzie, 1801, 151–2 and note; Masson, 1960, I, introduction:39). A Charles Cadien, probably the same man, was at Fort Chipewyan in 1799–1800 (Masson, 1960, II:379). In 1802–3, one Doucette was interpreter for James Leith, the XY Company trader on Peace River (PAM, Selkirk Papers, vol. 31, 9362; HBCA B.39/a/2, 38d); his first name is unknown.

DUCHAIN, JOSEPH, *milieu*, Athabasca, wages 300 *livres* (account pages 44d–45). This may be the "old Joseph" who engaged on 7 April 1786 to winter three years on Peace River (Journal). Duchain's wages, 300 *livres*, are among the lowest in the Account Book, a fact which is consistent with an older man near the end of his useful career.

DUMAS, PIERRE, *milieu*, Athabasca, wages 500 *livres* (account pages 26d–27). He engaged on 7 April 1786 to winter three years at Great Slave Lake (Journal; he is also mentioned on 6 and 22 April). A man of this name was hired by J.-Bte. Tabeau to go to the Mississippi in 1784 (APQ *Rapport*, 1946–7, 332); and a man of the same name was *commis* and interpreter for the North West Company in the Nipigon district in 1805 (Masson, 1960, I:407); although both are of about the right period, there is no other reason to assume that either is the man of the English River Book. Three voyageurs named Pierre Dumas are listed in the North West Company's great ledger for 1811–21. One, carried over from before 1811, served at Sault Ste Marie and retired in 1813; the second, hired in 1816, worked in Athabasca, and was part of Franklin's first Arctic expedition; and the third, hired in 1820, also worked in Athabasca (HBCA F.4/32, 322, 340, 252, respectively). The Hudson's Bay Company's roster of northern servants for 1821–2 lists a Pierre Dumas "A" at Athabasca, and a Pierre Dumas "B" at Lac La Pluie (HBCA B.239/g/1, 46, 42, respectively).

DURRELL *dit* MACTEM, FRANÇOIS, *milieu*, Athabasca, wages 550 *livres* (account pages 35d–36). Not mentioned in the Journal and no further information.

DURROCHER, JOSEPH, *gouvernail*, Île-à-la-Crosse and Lac La Ronge, wages 800 *livres* (account pages 43d–44; see also account of François Lafrance, 42d–43). A Joseph Durrocher was a voyageur at Lake Winnipeg in 1805 (Masson, 1960, 1:406), and one Jos. Durocher, probably the same, was guide for the same department in 1806 (Wallace, 1934, 220).

DUVALLE, PIERRE, *devant*, Athabasca, wages 800 *livres* (account pages 15d–16). Not mentioned in the Journal under this name, but probably the man referred to twice as "Pierish" (see below).

FANIANT, FRANÇOIS, *gouvernail*, Athabasca, wages 800 *livres* (account pages 46d–47). Mentioned in the Journal on 3, 13, and 25 April, he was the brother of Joseph Faniant or Fainant, according to his account. A François Fagnant was baptized at Île-Dupas in 1743, and the family later moved to Sorel (Tanguay, 1871–90, IV:4). A man of this name was hired by Pierre Cardinal in 1761 to go to Detroit (APQ *Rapport*, 1932–3, 261), and this may have been the man of the English River Book, at the start of his career.

FANIANT or FAINANT, JOSEPH, a Grand Portage guide, mentioned three times in the accounts in the English River Book. One entry (page 46d) shows that he was the brother of François Faniant, a *gouvernail* at Athabasca. In this and the other two references (38, 71d), Joseph Faniant was apparently acting as a voyageur's agent in transfers of money to Canada. John Macdonell in 1793 called him "Faignan ... a faithful servant and favorite of Jos. Frobisher Esq., for many years in the North west" (Gates, 1965, 68). In the light of this, and his involvement in transactions in the English River Book, it is likely that he was already a Grand Portage guide in 1785. Prior to his association with Frobisher, Faniant seems to have worked for J.E. Waddens when the latter was at Lac La Ronge in 1781–2, since he probably is the Joseph Faignant of Berthier who witnessed the shooting of Waddens and made a deposition to that effect at Montreal on 19 May 1783 (Davidson, 1967, 41 n; Wallace, 1954, 22–3). In the winter of 1791–2, John Gregory of the North West Company commissioned "St Cir & Faniant" to engage winterers for the company, and said "Fainiant is to Go Through the Different Parishes Round Him" (HBCA F.3/1, 29–30, Gregory to Simon McTavish,

Montreal 24 November 1791; St Cir is Pierre Saint-Cir, also a long-time Grand Portage guide). Writing from Grand Portage in 1792, Gregory reported that "Faniant is Arrived Safe," presumably with his brigade of Montreal canoes (Gregory to McTavish, Grand Portage, 5 August 1792, in McGill Libraries and Special Collections). Faniant was to have guided the North West Company brigade which left Lachine for Lake Superior on 27 May 1793, but Joseph Frobisher decided to keep him back for the June brigade (Gates, 1965, 68). In July 1800, William McGillivray wrote from Grand Portage that "Faniant leaves this with 8 Mackinac Canoes Containing 284 Packs – 5 Men in each" (NA MG19, B1–1, 144, McGillivray to McTavish, Frobisher & Co., Grand Portage, 19 July 1800).

FORCIER, JOSEPH, *milieu*, Île-à-la-Crosse, wages 500 *livres* (account pages 21d–22). A man of this name was hired by William Grant in 1778 to go to Pays Plat (Lake Superior) (APQ *Rapport*, 1932–3, 304). The Joseph Forcier who was a voyageur at Michipicoten and in the Nipigon country between 1816 and 1821 (HBCA F.4/32, 375), was probably a different man.

FORTIN, LOUIS, *gouvernail*, Île-à-la-Crosse, wages 800 *livres* (account pages 17d–18). William McGillivray intended to hire this man to summer at Rat River in 1790 (NA MG19, C1–4, 27). Fortin was *commis* at Rat River in 1805 (Masson, 1960, 1:405), but is not in the roster for 1806 (Wallace, 1934, 220), and had probably been retired in light of the excess of men available in the country after the coalition with the XY Company. Coues (1965, 951) has references to Fortin in the Rat River district in 1805–6, extracted from David Thompson's manuscript journals, including the observation, "old Fortin tipples."

GAGNIER, JEAN-BAPTISTE, *milieu*, Rat River, wages 550 *livres* (account pages 28d–29). No further information.

GRANT, CUTHBERT, probably Peter Pond's second-in-command at Athabasca in 1785–6, and almost certainly the author of the unsigned Journal in the English River Book. His name appears only once in the English River Book, in Joseph Preux's account, pages 19d–20. M.A. MacLeod and W.L. Morton (1974, 3), summarizing the results of unpublished research by Miss Evelyn Grant of Nairn,

Scotland, state that Cuthbert Grant was the brother of Robert Grant, one of the original partners of the North West Company, and reasonably suggest that Cuthbert entered the fur trade through his brother's agency. As noted in the introduction, he may have been responsible for introducing more detailed accounting practices into the English River district in 1785, and the brief check list of Cree words for trading goods, inside the front cover of the English River Book, may suggest that this was his first year in the northwest trade. Grant probably built a temporary post on the north shore of Lake Athabasca during the winter of 1785–6 and certainly occupied the important new post on the south shore of Great Slave Lake in the fall of 1786, opposed by Laurent Leroux for the New Concern. Notes on the Ezra Stiles copy of one of Pond's maps (reproduced in Davidson, 1967, 42) show that "Mr. Grant" determined the latitudes of both places, doubtless by the use of the quadrant, and David Thompson told Dr Bigsby that Cuthbert Grant had assisted Pond in making his maps of the northwest (Bigsby, 1969, 116). Grant was still in Athabasca in 1787–8 (Lamb, 1970, 431) but was placed in charge of another district (unnamed, but perhaps Swan River) in the fall of 1789 (Masson, 1960, 1:32), where he "made 120 packs and 8 Kegs castorum" (Lamb, 1970, 442). Cuthbert Grant is perhaps the "Mr Grant the Canadian Master" who opposed Charles Isham, the Hudson's Bay Company clerk at Swan River, in 1790–1 (HBCA B.213/a/1, 23 September 1790). Grant's station for the next two seasons is unknown (Peter Pangman was in charge at Swan River in 1791–2 and 1792–3 (HBCA B.213/a/2, 16 October 1791; B.213/a/3, 14 October 1792, 15 May 1793), though he may have been already on the upper part of the Assiniboine, the "Upper Red River" district.

Upon his brother Robert's retirement from the North West Company in the summer of 1793, Cuthbert Grant was put in charge of the Red River district (Gates, 1965, 96, 100, 102, 106, 112, 114; HBCA B.22/a/1, passim); he made his headquarters at Rivière Tremblante on the upper Assiniboine (Masson, 1960, 1:284–5). He remained in Red River in 1794–5 (Masson, 1960, 1:291–4; HBCA B.22/a/2, 17 September 1794), but fell seriously ill during the winter (Morton, 1929, 58; HBCA B.199/a/1, 15 January 1795). Probably he spent 1795–6 recovering his health in Canada or abroad; at any rate, William Thorburn is the only North West Company trader mentioned as in charge at Red River (HBCA B.22/a/3, 3 September 1795). In the fall of 1796 Cuthbert Grant and Thorburn were jointly in command of the district (HBCA B.22/a/4, 5 September 1796). Some reorganization evidently took place at the Grand Portage partners' meeting of 1796, since Grant was sent in to Red River by way of Lake Manitoba, Lake Winnipegosis, and Swan River, organizing posts in the Fort Dauphin district as he went though once again his headquarters were at Rivière Tremblante. [David Thompson followed Grant's route on this inward voyage, and his manuscript journals record the details of Grant's progress; see Coues, 1965, 164, 176, 299; Tyrrell, 1968b, lxxi–lxxii, 193–6. HBCA B.22/a/5, 8 September 1797, says that Thorburn "and Cuthbert Grant are the directors for Red River," but only Thorburn came in by the Assiniboine River route.] In the fall of 1798, Grant was sent to the Saskatchewan River to take the place of Angus Shaw, who was on furlough; renewed illness prevented him from working effectively, however, and he was brought down to Grand Portage, mortally sick, in the summer of 1799 and died there (Masson, 1960, II:23–4 and n). He left at least two sons and three daughters, one being Cuthbert Grant, the celebrated Métis leader (MacLeod and Morton, 1974).

Cuthbert Grant, the elder, was a partner of the North West Company by the spring of 1794, when he was addressed as such in a letter from the new corporate partners in Montreal (HBCA F.3/1, 151–2). He was not one of the four clerks who were made partners in 1793 (HBCA F.3/2, 16–17), and his partnership may have dated from 1791 or 1792.

GUY, JEAN-BAPTISTE, *milieu*, Île-à-la-Crosse, wages 500 *livres* (account pages 30d–31). There was a voyageur of this name at English River in 1805 (Masson, 1960, I:400).

GUYETTE, CHARLES, *gouvernail*, Rat River, wages 800 *livres* (account pages 35d–36). No further information.

GUYETTE, JOSEPH, *milieu*, Athabasca, wages 550 *livres* (account pages 33d–34). He, or the next, is mentioned in the Journal on 25 April.

GUYETTE, JOSEPH, D'YAMASKA, (so called to distinguish him from the previous man; account pages 19d–20; see also account of J.-B.

Rapin, 44d–45). His rank is not given but he had a *milieu's* wages, 500 *livres*; he was a new man in 1785. He came from Île-à-la-Crosse to Athabasca, doubtless with a letter from Patrick Small to Peter Pond, during the winter of 1785–6, and his account shows that he was paid 200 *livres* for the trip. He engaged on 10 April 1786 to winter three years in Peace River.

IRELANDE, BASILE, a Grand Portage guide, mentioned once in the English River Book accounts, that of Ambroise Lalonde (pages 49d–50), having been paid a small sum of Lalonde's behalf on 12 September 1786. Basile Riel, *dit* L'Irlande, was born at Lavaltrie, and baptized at the nearby parish of Saint-Sulpice in 1724 (Jetté, 1983, 985). Basile is frequently mentioned in the voyageurs' contracts in the period 1743–57, usually going to Michilimackinac, although once, in 1744, he was engaged for "la poste du Lac Bourbon," or Cedar Lake, Manitoba (APQ *Rapport*, 1929–30, 436, 446; 1922–3, 232; 1930–1, 360, 372, 386, 403, 423, 452; 1931–2, 293, 315, 328–9, 354). Most of these engagements were for summer trips, so that Basile would have spent his winters in Canada. He married Louise-Amable Boyer (probably the aunt of Charles Boyer, the Athabasca clerk of 1786), at Notre-Dame-de-Montréal in 1755 (Tanguay, 1871–90, II:446, VI:567). After the Conquest, Basile Irelande continued his association with the fur trade, and in 1769 he received a pass to take two canoes to Michilimackinac for Dobie and Frobisher (Morton Collection, Fur Trade Licences, 61). Further licences show him acting for the Frobishers and their partners taking canoes to Grand Portage in 1772, 1774, and 1775 (ibid., 223, 314, 374–5). He apparently continued to guide brigades for the Frobishers and the North West Company until at least 1793, when John Macdonell noted the arrival of "old Bazil Ireland the guide" at Grand Portage (Gates, 1965, 96). Several other members of the Riel *dit* L'Irlande family were voyageurs; one, Basile's great-nephew Jean-Baptiste, was the grandfather of Louis Riel (Tanguay, 1871–90, VI:567–8).

JOLLIE, PIERRE, a voyageur, apparently in English River in 1784–5, whose account was debited 60 *livres* in favour of Joseph Durrocher at the end of the 1784–5 season (see Durrocher's account pages 43d–44). The same man is presumably the Joly in whose favour Janvier Mayotte's account was debited 10 *livres* at the same time

(26d–27). Since no voyageur named Joly is in the 1785–6 accounts in the English River Book, this man must have been stationed elsewhere. "Pieire Jollie the Drunkard," with whom the North West Company partners were expected to be familiar, was a north guide for the newly formed XY Company in 1799 (Lamb, 1970, 489).

JOLYBOIS, FRANÇOIS, *gouvernail*, Athabasca, wages 800 *livres* (account pages 36Ad–36B). Mentioned in the Journal 22 April and 25 May. No further information.

LABONNE, —, an Athabasca voyageur mentioned in the journal on 6, 7 and 23 April. This name does not appear in the accounts and must be a nickname. Six men who seem, from their accounts, to have been stationed at Athabasca in 1785–6, are not mentioned in the *Journal* under their proper names. One, Pierre Duvalle, has been provisionally identified as the "Pierish" of the Journal. There seems to be no way to decide which of the five others – Raimond, Bodoin, Durrell *dit* Mactem, Maranda (who may be the "old Joseph" of the Journal), and Thesson – was Labonne.

LABRÊCHE, AMABLE (account pages 54d–55; his rank is not given). Placed on the English River books as a new man in 1785, he seems not to have reached the district, since no wages are shown for him. A man of this name was a North West Company voyageur at Athabasca in 1816–21 (HBCA F.4/32, 548).

LACHARITÉ, PIERRE, *milieu*, Île-à-la-Crosse, wages 390 *livres* (account pages 24d–25). A new man, with a new man's wages, in 1785. No further information.

LAFLEUR, JEAN-BAPTISTE, *milieu*, Athabasca, wages 400 *livres* (account pages 15d–16). Engaged on 14 April 1786 to winter three years at Peace River, he was also mentioned in the Journal on 24 April and 6 May. This man, and later his son and namesake, are familiar figures in North West Company documents relating to the fur trade on Peace River. The father was a summer man at Fort Chipewyan in 1791 and 1793 (Lamb, 1970, 445, 451), had probably built Fort Vermilion, Peace River, by 1800 (see Wallace, 1929, 55), interpreted for Simon Fraser at Fort Liard (Peace River) in 1802–3 (Selkirk Papers, vol. 32, 9362), and was interpreter at Fort Vermilion in 1806 (Wallace, 1929, 122–34). He appears in the 1806 North West Company roster as J.B. La Fleur Senior, interpreter at Athabasca (Wallace, 1934, 219). The great North West Company ledger for 1811–21 shows him with wages of 500 *livres* for 1811–15 and 1816–21 – he seems to have been in Canada for the season of 1815–16 (HBCA F.4/32, 490). His last contract with the North West Company is preserved in HBCA. It was concluded at "Fort de la Grande Prairie dans la Riviere la Paix" on 17 April 1819, with John George McTavish acting for the company, and stipulated that "J.Bte. Lafleur Sen." was to winter for two years on Peace River as an interpreter, for 500 *livres* "argent de Grand Portage," plus other specified perquisites. The contract was renewed for one more year in 1821 (HBCA F.5/3, 38). Lafleur, his son Jean-Baptiste, and a Michel Lafleur who may be another son all retired to Canada in 1822 (HBCA B.239/g/2, 55).

Jean-Baptiste Lafleur *fils*, born about 1786, was also an interpreter at Athabasca in 1806, when he was stationed at Dunvegan on Peace River (Wallace, 1929, 122–34; 1934, 219). He is the "Baptiste" who was Harmon's interpreter at Dunvegan in 1809 (Harmon, 1973, 147). The younger Lafleur was employed by the North West Company in Athabasca during the entire period 1811–21, with steadily increasing wages (HBCA F.4/32, 490), was taken over by the Hudson's Bay Company in 1821, but, as already noted, retired to Canada with his father in 1822. His last North West Company contract was concluded on 9 May 1821. By it Lafleur was to winter on Peace River as an interpreter, at 1000 *livres* plus miscellaneous items. Most revealing is the concluding sentence: "le dit Compagnie s'oblige a lui donner dans leurs canots a passage a Montreal avec ses familles, et Son Pere passeras l'hiver avec lui" (HBCA F.5/3, 39). As already noted, the Lafleurs went down to Montreal in 1822. Lafleur *fils* was rehired for Athabasca in 1827 (HBCA B.239/g/6, 16), and remained as an interpreter on Peace River until 1875 (HBCA A.32/37, 89; B.235/g/3, 36), when he is said to have died at the age of 90 (Wallace, 1929, 55). His son Baptiste Lafleur was also an interpreter on Peace River (Wallace, 1929, 55), and had several children who are listed in the 1881 census of Canada (District 192–S, 3).

LAFRANCE, FRANÇOIS (account pages 42d–43; no rank given). According to his account he died at Île-à-la-Crosse in summer 1785.

The Frobishers owed £46/7/1, Halifax currency, to one François La France in 1787, but this debt was "effaced" as part of the division of debts when the firm of McTavish, Frobisher & Co was formed in that year (Wallace, 1934, 81). One François La France retired from the fur trade with 12,000 *livres* to his credit in 1791 (Lamb, 1970, 448). Yet another Lafrance, apparently a financial agent for Brousseau and Ledoux (see their accounts), has not been identified.

LALIBERTÉ, NICHOLAS, *milieu*, Lac La Ronge, wages 400 *livres* (account pages 52d–53), a new man in 1785. No further information.

LALONDE, AMBROISE, *gouvernail*, Athabasca, wages 800 *livres* (account pages 49d–50). He was mentioned in the Journal, 22 April. Although he was not in the Upper Country in 1784–5, his rank shows that he was an experienced canoeman. He was probably the Ambroise Lalande who was baptized in 1752 at Sainte-Geneviève-de Montréal (Tanguay, 1871–90, v:98). A man of this name, again probably the same, was hired by Hypolite Desrivières in 1769 to go to Michilimackinac (APQ *Rapport*, 1932–3, 292).

LANDRIEFFE, JOSEPH, *gouvernail*, Athabasca, wages 800 *livres* (account pages 23d–24). His surname is spelled inconsistently in the two entries in the Journal which mention him: he is Landrie on 6 April (when he arrived from what may have been his winter station on Lake Athabasca), and Landriefe on 7 April when he hired for three years to winter at Great Slave Lake. This may be the name Tanguay spells Landrière (Tanguay, 1871–90, v:127). He may have been one of the five voyageurs who drowned in Slave River in the fall of 1786 (introduction, page xxxvii).

LANDRY *dit* CADIEN, JOSEPH, *gouvernail*, Athabasca, wages 800 *livres* (account pages 15d–16, which spells his name Landrie). He engaged on 3 April 1786 to winter three years at Great Slave Lake. (For his nickname, which means *acadien*, see Charles Doucette.) A Joseph Landry was hired in 1772 by Louis Réaume to go to Michilimackinac (APQ *Rapport*, 1932–3, 300); and a Jo. Landry was among the canoemen listed on an Indian trade licence issued to James McGill and Charles Paterson, apparently in 1774, to take five canoes and thirty-four men to Grand Portage (Morton Collection, Fur Trade Licences, 334). Joseph Landry and Charles Doucette both accompanied Alexander Mackenzie to the Arctic Ocean in 1789 and to the Pacific in 1793, and Mackenzie's steersman, who had been with him for five years in 1793, was probably the *gouvernail* Landry (Mackenzie, 1801, 358).

LANGUEDOCQUE, JEAN-BAPTISTE, *milieu*, Athabasca, wages 500 *livres* (account pages 14d–15). Mentioned in the Journal as Langdeau on 9 April. No further information.

LAPRISE, JEAN-BAPTISTE, *milieu*, Athabasca, wages 500 *livres* (account pages 17d–18; see also Coté's account, 37d–38). He engaged on 3 April 1786 to winter three years at Great Slave Lake (Journal), and later references all place him there or on the Mackenzie River. In 1799 he was hired at Fort Chipewyan by Roderick McKenzie to work four years as a *gouvernail* in "les Pays des Esclaves," wages 400 *livres* (HBCA F.5/1, 11). He brought letters from Great Slave Lake to Fort Chipewyan on 31 January 1800 (Masson, 1960, II:380). The following summer, accompanied by his two wives, he took charge of the North West Company's Mackenzie River fort until the arrival of the master, John Thomson (Thomson's Rocky Mountain Fort journal, HBCA Copy No. 124, 4). Laprise was with Wentzel at the "Grand River" (the Mackenzie) post in 1805–6 (PAM, Selkirk Papers, vol. 31, 9298–9308). In 1806 J.B. Laprise was an interpreter in Athabasca (Wallace, 1934, 219), but he is not in the North West Company's ledger of 1811–21 (HBCA F.4/32) and probably had died or retired. An Indian called "LaPrise's son-in-law" traded with John Stuart and Wentzel in August 1800 on Peace River (NA MG19, C1–15, 23), a fact which seems to show that Laprise had fathered at least one daughter in the northwest by the late 1780s. The Chipewyan Métis, Baptiste La Prise, a freeman who figured prominently in Samuel Black's Finlay River expedition of 1824 (Rich, 1955, 221–2), was probably the elder Jean-Baptiste's son.

LARIVIÈRE, FRANÇOIS, *devant*, Athabasca, wages 800 *livres* (account pages 36Bd–37). Mentioned in the Journal on 23 and 25 April and 8 May. A man of this name, perhaps the same, was hired by Ignace Hubert Lacroix in 1761 to go to Michilimackinac (APQ *Rapport*,

1932–3, 265). François Larivière was an interpreter at English River in 1805 (Masson, 1960, 1:399), but is not in the 1806 roster (Wallace, 1934, 219–21), and probably retired in the summer of 1806.

LAVALLÉ, IGNACE, *gouvernail*, Île-à-la-Crosse, wages 800 *livres* (account pages 41d–42; see also the accounts of Alexis Boyé, 24d–25, and Augustin Piccott, 30d–31). A child of this name was baptized at Saint-Pierre-de-Sorel in 1764, the son of Michel Lavalée and Marie-Joseph Millet; the surname Lavallé is very common at Sorel in the eighteenth century. There was a voyageur named Ignace Lavallée at English River in 1805 (Masson, 1960, 1:400); he is probably the man of the name who was employed by the North West Company during 1811–21 (HBCA F.4/32, 534), and was on the Hudson's Bay Company's list of Northern Department servants for 1821–2 (HBCA B.239/g/1, 59), but not later. All these references may be to the Ignace Lavallée of the English River Book. An Ignace Lavallée, probably still the same, died at Red River in 1836, at the supposed age of seventy-six; his wife Josephte was a Cree, and they had two sons, Baptiste and Pierre Lavallée, who also lived at Red River (Sprague and Frye, 1983, table 1, ID nos. 2806, 2810, 2819; Lareau and Hamelin, 1984, entry no. 11079).

LAVALLÉ, JEAN-BAPTISTE, *gouvernail*, Île-à-la-Crosse, wages 800 *livres* (account pages 18d–19). In 1805 Jean-Baptiste Lavallé, Sr, was an interpreter at English River, while Jean-Baptiste Lavallé, Jr, presumably his son, was a voyageur in the same district (Masson, 1960, 1:399–400). Two men of this name appear in the North West Company's ledger of men's accounts for 1811–21 but neither was at English River: one was stationed mainly at Lac La Pluie, while the other came up from Montreal in 1815 and was stationed at Michipi-coten (HBCA F.4/32, 592, 640).

LAVERDURE, JOSEPH, *milieu*, Athabasca, wages 550 *livres* (account pages 23d–24). He engaged on 7 April 1786 to winter three years at Great Slave Lake, and is also mentioned in the Journal on 6 and 22 April. A man of this name was one of twenty-two hired in June 1768 to go to various posts around Lake Michigan (APQ *Rapport*, 1932–3, 291; the name of the employer is not given). A Laverdure, probably the same, carried a letter from Roderick McKenzie to

Alexander Mackenzie in November 1788 (Lamb, 1970, 435). A Joseph Laverdure, voyageur, was at English River in 1805 (Masson, 1960, 1:400), Joseph Laverdure, likely the same, was married to an Indian woman named Lisette; their son Joseph settled at Red River (Sprague and Frye, 1983, table 1, ID nos. 2837, 2840). This son may have been the Métis Joseph Laverdure who came up from Montreal in 1817 as a North West Company engagé but was "dismissed the service" (HBCA F.4/32, 572).

LAVIOLETTE, FRANÇOIS, *milieu*, Athabasca, wages 550 *livres* (account pages 45d–46; see also account of François Piché, 36AD–36B). He engaged on 3 April 1786 to winter three years at Great Slave Lake; he is also mentioned in the Journal on 15 April. A Laviolette, likely the same, was at Fort Chipewyan in 1799–1800 (Masson, 1960, II:391–2, 394), and on Mackenzie River in 1800–1 (John Thomson's Rocky Mountain Fort Journal, HBCA Copy No. 124).

LEBLANC, FRANÇOIS, *devant*, Lac La Ronge, wages 800 *livres* (account pages 20d–21; see also account of François Monette, 31d–32). No further information.

LEDOUX, DOMINIQUE, *milieu*, Athabasca, wages 550 *livres* (account pages 21d–22). Engaged on 3 April 1786 to winter three years at Great Slave Lake (Journal). He may have been one of the five voyageurs drowned on Slave River in the fall of 1786 (see introduction, page xxxvii).

LEPIN, FRANÇOIS, *milieu* (account pages 33d–34). In English River 1784–5, he did not return the next season. A François Lépine, perhaps the same, was a voyageur at Rat River in 1805 (Masson, 1960, 1:405).

LESIEUR, TOUSSAINT (account pages 55d–56), probably Patrick Small's second-in-command at Île-à-la-Crosse in 1785–6. He may have been in charge at Lac La Ronge, which was manned by five voyageurs in this season, but there is no evidence. He must be the Toussaint, sixth child of Charles Lesieur and Ursule Du Parl-Bouvier, who was baptized at Yamachiche in 1754 (Tanguay, 1871–90, V:371; members of this family, including Toussaint's grandfather, were seigneurs of Yamaska). Lesieur first appears as Peter Pond's clerk at Lac La Ronge in 1781–2, when he was implicated in the death of Waddens (Davidson, 1967, 41 and n). He apparently returned to Canada, since he was arrested for this crime (see introduction, page xvii), but returned to English River in 1785 as the Account Book shows. His contract with Benjamin and Joseph Frobisher "pour aller aux postes de la rivière aux Anglais" was not registered in Montreal until 30 March 1786 (APQ *Rapport*, 1946–7, 354). Lesieur was left in charge at Île-à-la-Crosse for the summer of 1786, as the inventory on page 60d of the English River Book shows, and the next autumn he seems to have established a new post up the Beaver River, opposed for the New Concern by Louis Versailles. This, at least, is an interpretation of Alexander Mackenzie's report: "I sent off Versaille for the Beaver River, seven days ago with five of my best men. I expect he will make as well out as the famous Lisseur" (Lamb, 1970, 423). William Tomison of the Hudson's Bay Company, writing from the upper Saskatchewan this season, noted that he had dealt with "one tent of Indians arrived from the Beaver River... having just come from two Houses that has been erected this fall at the aforementioned River" (HBCA B.121/a/1, 11 January 1787). We next hear of Lesieur in 1789–90, when he was said to have taken over the trade at "the post of Rivière des Trembles and Portage de l'Île" (the east side of Lake Winnipeg and the Winnipeg River, respectively) in partnership with Simon Fraser (Masson, 1960, I:32). This partnership agreement was extended for five years more in 1791, though Lesieur himself went down to Canada for the sake of his health (Lamb, 1970, 448). In 1792, having returned to the Indian Country, he built a new post at Bas-de-la-Rivière (the foot of the Winnipeg River), which was to become an important provisioning post for the northwest canoe brigades (Gates, 1965, 107). Lesieur was trading at Bas-de-la-Rivière in 1793–4 and 1794–5 (HBCA B.166/a/1, 11 November 1793, 2 February 1794; B.166/a/2, 24 June and 19 August 1794), but was not there in either of the next two seasons (HBCA B.4/a/1, 28 September 1795; B.236/a/1, 9 September 1796, 23 January 1797). In the fall of 1794, Joseph Frobisher had anticipated that Lesieur would claim a partnership in the North West Company (HBCA F.3/1, 204, J. Frobisher to S. McTavish, Montreal 8 November 1794), but an agreement between Lesieur and the company's agents, McTavish, Frobisher & Co, signed early in 1796, seems to have ended Lesieur's participation in the fur trade (ANQ-M, CN1–29 [Étude Beek], 14 January 1794, doc. 1016). The Toussaint Le Sueur who was a clerk for the North West Company at Grandes Fourches, Red River (now Grand Forks, North Dakota) in 1805–6, and seems to have returned to Canada the following summer (Masson, 1:401; Coues, 1965, 267, 276), may have been the elder Toussaint's son.

LETENDRE, JEAN-BAPTISTE, *devant*, Rat River, wages 800 *livres* (account pages 13d–14). The Letendre family was well established at Sorel in the eighteenth century, and there were several Jean-Baptistes. This man may have been the J.B. Letendre who was engaged in 1757 by Sr Charles Lefebvre, and in 1761 by Ignace Hubert Lacroix, to go to Michilimackinac (APQ *Rapport*, 1931–2, 345; 1932–3, 266). Alternatively, he may have been a younger man, born at Sorel in 1762, whose biography is given by Payment (1987). If all her references are to the same individual, this Letendre, *dit* Batoche, may be traced as a freeman on the Saskatchewan and later at Red River between 1804 and 1827. It was the grandson of this man, according to Payment, who founded the village of Batoche on the South Saskatchewan in 1872.

L'EUNEAU, JEAN-MARIE, *milieu*, Rat River, wages 500 *livres* (account pages 27d–28). No further information.

MARANDA, JOSEPH, *milieu*, Athabasca, wages 500 *livres* (account pages 27d–28). Not mentioned in the Journal unless he is the "old Joseph" referred to at 7 April. One Joseph Moran *dit* Grimard was engaged by Louis Réaume in 1772 to go to the *pays d'en haut* (APQ *Rapport*, 1932–3, 300). The North West Company great ledger for 1811–21 has accounts for two men of this name: Joseph Maranda, in Athabasca 1811–21, and Joseph Morand, at Rat River in 1811–12 and Cumberland House 1812–15 (HBCA F.4/32, 652, 673). Both accounts had been carried over from before 1811, and one of them may be the same as the English River *engagé* of 1786. There was also a voyageur named Jos Marandas at Fond du Lac in 1805 (Masson, 1960, 1:410), who is probably not the same.

MARCILLE, PIERRE, *milieu*, Athabasca, wages 500 *livres* (account pages 16d–17). He is mentioned in the Journal on 6 and 23 April 1786. He is probably the Pierre Marsil who was baptized at Longueuil in 1738 (Tanguay, 1871–90, v:526) and was listed as a canoe-man on a *congé* granted in 1752 to Sr Damours de Clignancour for trade at Rivière Saint-Joseph (APQ *Rapport,* 1922–3, 263). He was hired in 1771 by Alexis Séjourné to go to Michilimackinac (APQ *Rapport,* 1932–3, 299). Several references place him still at Atha-basca in 1800. James Mackenzie calls him "old Marcil" in his Fort Chipewyan journal of 1799–1800 (Masson, 1960, II:385). He was hired in 1800 at Fort Chipewyan to work as a *milieu* "dans les Terres" – that is, not to work in the brigade to and from Lac La Pluie – at Grand Lac (Great Slave Lake), wages 300 *livres* (HBCA F.5/1, 24). Marcille was with Wentzel on Peace River the following summer, according to Wentzel's journal fragment of June-August 1800. Wentzel was not impressed by his enterprise (NA MG19, C1–15, passim; I am indebted to Mary Black-Rogers for this reference). A Cree Indian named Charlo Marcille, who traded with the Hudson's Bay Company at Fort Chipewyan in 1822 (HBCA B.39/a/20, 12d, 30 August 1822), was likely a son or grandson of Pierre Marcille.

MARTIN, SIMON, *devant,* Athabasca, wages 800 *livres* (account pages 32d–33). Mentioned in the Journal on 24 April and 6 and 21 May 1786. One Martin was with Roderick McKenzie on the north shore of Great Slave Lake in 1790–1 (Lamb, 1970, 444). One Martin, with his wife, was with John Thomson on the Mackenzie River in 1800–1 (Thomson's Rocky Mountain Fort journal, HBCA Copy No. 124 passim). "Old Martin" was with Wentzel on the Mackenzie in 1805–6 (PAM, Selkirk Papers, vol. 31, 9298–9308). All of these references may be to Simon Martin.

MAYÉ, PIERRE, *milieu,* Île-à-la-Crosse, wages 375 *livres* (account pages 53d–54). A new man in 1785. A Pre. Mayet is listed as a canoeman for the Frobishers in 1772 (Morton Collection, Fur Trade Licences, 223).

MAYOTTE, JANVIER, Athabasca, wages 600 *livres* (account pages 26d–27; his rank is not given, but he may have been an interpreter, since his wages were above those for most *milieux*). He is mentioned in the Journal on 3 and 13 April 1786. This is probably the Janvier Mayat who was one of 26 men engaged by Dobie and Frobisher to take three canoes to Michilimackinac and Grand Portage in 1770 (Morton Collection, Fur Trade Licences, 117).

MESSIER, CHARLES, *milieu*, Île-à-la-Crosse, wages 500 *livres* (account pages 43d–44, see also account of Piccott, 30d–31). Alexander Mackenzie hoped to hire him as summer interpreter for Rat River in 1788 (Lamb, 1970, 434). He is probably the Messier whom William McGillivray left in charge of the Lac La Ronge post in March, 1790, while McGillivray was off getting Indian credits (NA MG19, C1–4, 24d). Charles Messier was in charge of a North West Company outfit which traded in Rat River in 1794–5, opposed by George Charles, the Hudson's Bay Company's trader at Granville House (HBCA B.83/a/1, 25 September 1794). Messier is listed as an interpreter at Rat River in 1797–8 (PAC *Report*, 1939, 55), and was in Lower English River (which included Rat River in that season) in 1799, wages 600 *livres* (Masson, 1960, 1:62). He is not in the 1805 list of North West Company employees (Masson, 1960, 1:395–413), and had perhaps retired. He may well be the Charles Messier, married to Marie-Joseph Adam, whose two daughters were baptized at Saint-Pierre-de-Sorel in 1816 and 1819.

MODESTE, ANTOINE, *milieu*, Rat River, wages 400 *livres* (account pages 34d–35). A new man in 1785.

MONETTE, FRANÇOIS, guide, Île-à-la-Crosse, wages 1000 *livres* (account pages 31d–32; see also Leblanc's account, 20d–21). A man of this name and his son Michel were hired in 1765 by Abraham Cuyler and Stephen Groesbak to go to Michilimackinac (APQ *Rapport*, 1932–3, 282). Monette, the father, may then have been the Louis-François Monet who was baptized at Montreal in 1718, married Félicité Morel at Lachine in 1741, and with her had four children, including Michel, baptized at Sainte-Geneviève-de-Montréal in 1745 (Tanguay, 1871–90, VI:67–8; Charbonneau and Légaré, 1980–5, XXV:320). Félicité Morel was the aunt of one of the English River *devants* of 1786, Jean-Baptiste Rapin (see below). If François Monette, the Île-à-la-Crosse guide, was indeed her husband, he would have been sixty-seven years old in 1786, and in any case he probably retired soon after, since Jean-Baptiste Antaya was the English River guide by 1791.

NADOT, FRANÇOIS, *milieu*, Île-à-la-Crosse, wages 375 *livres* (account pages 38d–39; see also accounts of Piccott, 30d–31, and Lafrance, 42d–43). A new man in 1785, in 1786–7 he was apparently reassigned to Athabasca, for a document cited by Wagner (1955, 45 n 26) reports the trial of "François Nadeau and Eustache Le Comte for the murder of John Ross at Arabasca." Le Comte is not in the English River Book and must have been a new man in 1786–7. Nadot was hired on 23 June 1788 by Eustache Beaubien Desrivières to go to Témiscamingue (APQ, *Rapport*, 1946–7, 367).

NASPLETTE *dit* PASS-PAR-TOUT, JOSEPH, Athabasca, wages 550 *livres* (account pages 16d–17; his rank is not given, but his salary was that of an experienced *milieu* or other useful man; he may have been an interpreter). He engaged on 7 April 1786 to winter three years at Great Slave Lake (Journal). He was perhaps a son of Michel Nasplaise *dit* Passe-partout, a soldier of the Royal Roussillon regiment, who was married at Verchères in 1760 (Tanguay, 1871–90, VI:136). One Nasplette, probably Joseph, was at Dunvegan on Peace River in 1806 (Wallace, 1929, 122–34), and 1808 (PAM, Selkirk Papers, vol. 31, 9274–81). A Joseph Nasplette, again probably the same, was employed in Athabasca by the North West Company in 1811–20, wages 400 *livres* in 1812–14 and 300 *livres* thereafter; he was retired in the summer of 1820 (HBCA F.4/32, 753). The Indian named Paspeetoo or Paspertoo who traded with Peter Fidler at Nottingham House, Lake Athabasca, in the spring of 1803 (HBCA B.39/a/2, 47, d), may have been a Métis son of Nasplette.

PAGÉ, ANTOINE, *devant*, Lac La Ronge, wages 800 *livres* (account pages 37d–38). He was a *commis* and interpreter at English River in 1805 (Masson, 1960, I:399), but is not in the 1806 roster of North West Company clerks and interpreters (Wallace, 1934, 219–21) and had perhaps been retired. Another Antoine Payet or Paget was with Alexander Henry the younger at Lower Red River in 1802–5 (Coues, 1965, 204, 226, 249, 250). The Antoine Pagé who was on the company books as owing money in 1811 but no longer earning wages (HBCA F.4/32, 797), may have been either of these.

PAPAN, CHARLES, *milieu*, Athabasca, wages 550 *livres* (account pages 22d–23). He engaged on 14 April 1786 to winter three years at Peace River (Journal; he is also mentioned on 24 April). Charles Papin *dit* Lachance was engaged by the Frobishers on 20 February 1784 to go to Grand Portage (APQ *Rapport*, 1946–7, 331). He was perhaps the Charles Pepin *dit* Lachance who was baptized at Quebec in 1763 (Tanguay, 1871–90, VI:300).

PAPAN, JOSEPH, *milieu*, Île-à-la-Crosse, wages 500 *livres* (account pages 20d–21; see also accounts of Antoine Bourcier, 13d–14, and Ignace Lavallé, 41d–42). A Jos. Papin, perhaps the same, was a voyageur at English River in 1805 (Masson, 1960, 1:400). Two men of this name appear in the North West Company's great ledger for 1811–21. Joseph Papan, whose account was carried over from before 1811, earned a modest 200 *livres* per year in 1811–14 in the Nipigon district and then retired. Joseph Peppin was at Fort William in 1818–19 but deserted in the spring of 1819 (HBCA F.4/32, 816, 1002). The Joseph Pepin who contracted with William Grant on 31 January 1786 to go to Michilimackinac, and again on 15 February to go to the Mississippi (APQ *Rapport*, 1946–7, 350, 353), must have been a different man, since our subject was in English River at the time.

PARISIEN, BONAVAN, *devant*, Île-à-la-Crosse, wages 800 *livres* (account pages 39d–40). Alexander Mackenzie referred to Parisien as an "able foreman," and hoped to borrow him for the Athabasca brigade in September 1787 (Lamb, 1970, 427). A man of this name, probably the same, was at Fort des Prairies in 1805 (Masson, 1960, 1:399) and also in 1811–17, wages 400 *livres* in 1812–15 and 200 *livres* (an old man's salary) in 1817–18, dying at Fort des Prairies on 24 November 1817 (HBCA F.4/32, 794). He was probably the father of the Metis, Bonaventure Parisien, who died at Red River in 1867, said to have been aged seventy. The younger Bonaventure is supposed to have had three sons by 1810 (Sprague and Frye, 1983, table 1, ID. nos 3823, 3829, 3833 and 3841), but in view of his age it seems likelier that these were sons of Bonaventure Parisien the elder.

PASS-PAR-TOUT, see Nasplette *dit* Pass-par-tout, Joseph.

PERRAULT, JOSEPH, *milieu*, Athabasca, wages 550 *livres* (account pages 25d–26). He engaged on 3 April 1786 to winter three years at Great Slave Lake (Journal). He was hired as a *devant* at Fort Chipewyan on 29 April 1801 (HBCA F.5/1, 32).

PICCOTT or PICOTÉ, AUGUSTIN, Athabasca, wages 300 *livres* (account pages 30d–31, rank not given; see also Ignace Lavallé's account, 41d–42). He was not in English River in 1784–5, and his wages were those of an inexperienced man, but he acted as a *devant* for one of the outward bound Athabasca canoes in May 1786 (Journal, 8 May). These facts seem to indicate that he was actually an experienced man but near the end of his useful years as a voyageur. He engaged on 25 April 1786 to winter three years at Athabasca Fort. If the suggestion about his age is correct, he was probably the Augustin Picot who was baptized at Repentigny in 1730, the son of Pierre Picot and Marie-Madeleine Brussau (Charbonneau and Légaré, 1980–5, XXVI:112). A man of this name, probably the same, engaged in 1759 with Dejordy de Villebon, the last French commander of the western posts, to go to "La Mer du Ouest" (Lake Winnipeg or beyond), and in 1762 with Antoine Janise & Cie to go to Michilimackinac (APQ *Rapport*, 1932–3, 254, 269). With the possible exception of François Monette, Augustin Piccott was probably the most experienced voyageur in English River in 1786. The Augustin Picotte who worked for the North West Company on Athabasca River in 1817–21 (HBCA F.4/32, 786), was evidently a much younger man.

PICHÉ, FRANÇOIS, *devant*, Athabasca, wages 800 *livres* (account 36Ad–36B; see also Laviolette's account, 45d–46). He was mentioned in the Journal on 6 May 1786, when he and Rapin arrived with a letter from Patrick Small at Île-à-la-Crosse. Since Piché also used the nickname La Mesette, he was probably a member of the family Pichet *dit* Lamusette of Lavaltrie and Repentigny (Tanguay, 1871–90, VI:351–2). This man was probably the François Pichet who hired with William and John Kay in 1778, to go to Michilimackinac, and the François Piché who hired with Richard Dobie in 1782 to go to the same place (APQ *Rapport*, 1946–7, 308, 317). He is said to have been the actual killer of John Ross at Athabasca in the spring of 1787 (see introduction, page xxiii). After the death of Ross, Piché fled to the Chipewyans, where he remained three years, afraid of the gallows but in the summer of 1790 he was in charge of the North West Company's post on Great Slave Lake (Tyrrell, 1968a, 394 n, 417 and n). On 21 January 1799 "François La Mesette dit Peché" was hired at Fort Chipewyan for five years, at 500 *livres* per annum, as "commis interprete boute &c" to serve anywhere "Lac la Merde exempt" (Lac La Martre is meant; HBCA F.5/1, 8). In 1799–1800 Piché was at Fort Chipewyan, and James McKenzie's journal of that season has something to say about his character (Masson, 1960, II:392, 395–7). The following summer, apparently, "Pichés" located the site for a new North West Company fort on the Mackenzie River, below the mouth of the Liard (John Thomson's Rocky Mountain Fort journal, HBCA Copy No. 124, 5–6). He was stationed at a North West Company fort on or near Great Slave Lake in the summer of 1802, as appears from Wentzel's journal for that season (McGill Libraries and Special Collections). Piché was in charge of the main Mackenzie River post in the summer of 1806, along with one "Gadoies," and served as interpreter there the following winter (PAM, Selkirk Papers, vol. 31, 9340–50). In the North West Company's arrangement of departments for 1806 he appears as F. Lamisette, interpreter at Athabasca (Wallace, 1934, 219). He is not in the North West Company's great ledger of men's accounts for 1811–21 and must have retired or died; the François Piché who was at English River in 1819–21 (HBCA F.4/32, 1077), was evidently a younger man. Métis employees of the Hudson's Bay Company named Piché in Athabasca in the 1820s were probably sons of the elder François Piché.

PIERISH, an Athabasca voyageur mentioned in the Journal on 12 April and 9 May. On the latter occasion, he had the misfortune to throw Cuthbert Grant's gun into the Athabasca River while hoisting a canoe sail, presumably by entangling the gun in the rope. This name is not in the Account Book, and must be a nickname for someone else. Dr Mary Black-Rogers has found the name Pierish as a disapproving diminutive for Pierre Saint-Germain in Athabasca in the 1820s. Of the four Pierres at Athabasca, Bellanger, Dumas, and Marcille are all mentioned in the Journal under these names, in contexts which do not permit confusion with Pierish; thus, by elimination, Pierish was the *devant*, Pierre Duvalle, whose account shows that he was at Athabasca although he is not mentioned under this name in the Journal. This identification in turn shows that Duvalle was the *devant* in charge of the last canoe to leave Athabasca Fort in May 1786.

POND, PETER, in command at Athabasca in 1785–6, and mentioned several times in the Journal. The biographical article on Pond by

Gough (1983) is a comprehensive account of current knowledge and a guide to the sources; see also the introduction, pages xv-xxiv.

PREUX, JOSEPH, *devant*, Athabasca, wages 800 *livres* (account pages 19d–20). He is mentioned in the Journal at 20 April, and 7 and 11 May, and his "woman" is referred to in his account. A Joseph Proux was hired by Pierre Leduc in 1761 to go to Michilimackinac (APQ *Rapport*, 1932–3, 266), and a Joseph Proulx was hired by James Grant in 1784, to go to Témiscamingue (APQ *Rapport*, 1946–7, 341). Since the account of Joseph Preux in the English River Book shows a debit balance carried over from 1784–5, he was in that district in that season, and the man who hired for Témiscamingue must have been someone else.

PREUX, PIERRE, *milieu*, Île-à-la-Crosse, wages 500 *livres* (account pages 14d–15). No further information.

PRIMEAU, PAUL, Rat River, wages 400 *livres* (account pages 34d–35; called "Monsieur," and thus a *commis* or clerk). He may be the Paul Primeau who was baptized at Quebec in 1763 (Tanguay, 1871–90, VI:452); he was engaged by the Frobishers on 11 February 1784 to go to Grand Portage (APQ *Rapport*, 1946–7, 329). This is evidently the Primeau who spent the summer at Rat River in 1786, although Malchom Ross, the Hudson's Bay Company servant who was travelling through the district, assumed that "Primo" was the sometime Hudson's Bay Company employee, Louis Primot (see biography of Jurial Baldwin). Paul Primeau does not appear in the fur trade literature again, and probably soon returned to Canada. He may be the man of this name who married Marie-Joseph Bureau at Quebec on 6 February 1798 (Tanguay, 1871–90, VI:452).

QUISSON, —, *gouvernail*, Athabasca, wages 700 *livres* (account pages 50d–51). Not in English River in 1784–5, since no balance is carried over in his account, he was mentioned in the Journal on 4 May. No further information.

RAIMOND, FRANÇOIS, *devant*, Athabasca, wages 900 *livres* (account pages 47d–48). His account records a charge against him of 100 *livres* for "passage of his woman." A man of this name was hired by Ezekiel Solomon on 17 May 1779 to go to Pays Plat (the rendezvous for the Nipigon trade, on the north shore of Lake Superior) (APQ *Rapport*, 1946–7, 312). One F. Raymond was a voyageur at English River in 1805 (Masson, 1960, I:400).

RAIMOND, PIERRE DE, Île-à-la-Crosse, wages 300 *livres* (account pages 49d–50; his rank is not given; see also accounts of Antoine Bourcier, 13d–14, and Antoine Tourangeau, 38d–39). His low wages and unspecified rank suggest that he was an older man, no longer expected to work in canoes, but I have no further information.

RAPIN, JEAN-BAPTISTE, *devant*, Île-à-la-Crosse and Athabasca, wages 800 *livres* (account pages 44d–45; see also accounts of Lafleur, 15d–16, Joseph Guyette d'Yamaska, 19d–20, Coté, 37d–38, and Bruillete, 45d–46). The record in his account of two payments from Île-à-la-Crosse voyageurs (Coté and Joseph Guyette d'Yamaska), and the fact that most of his winter charges were in the Île-à-la-Crosse book, suggest that he spent much of 1785–6 at Île-à-la-Crosse. He arrived at Athabasca Fort with François Piché on 6 May 1786, bringing a letter from Patrick Small to Pond, and was engaged on that date to serve three years inland (Journal). Probably he was originally assigned to Île-à-la-Crosse and was sent up to Athabasca to help with the summer expeditions planned to settle new posts on Great Slave Lake and Peace River, in response to the opposition of the New Concern. Rapin's name is rare and distinctive, and he is probably to be identified with Jean-Baptiste Rapin, son of Jean-Baptiste Rapin, *commerçant*, and Catherine Morel, who was born at Lachine in 1748 (Charbonneau and Légaré, 1980–5, XXV:509). Catherine Morel's sister Félicité was the wife of François Monet, possibly to be identified with the English River guide of 1785–6 (ibid., 302; see his biography), and two of the younger Jean-Baptiste Rapin's sisters married members of the fur trading family of Hubert *dit* Lacroix (Tanguay, 1871–90, VI:509). A Jean-Baptiste Rapin took a canoe of goods to Michilimackinac for Peter Bouthillier in 1769, and took another to Grand Portage on his own security in 1770 (Morton Collection, Fur Trade Licences, 47, 119). These two items are likelier to refer to the father than the son, who was barely twenty-one years old in 1769, but the son was probably the "Bte Rapin" who is listed as a canoeman on the licence for the latter expedition.

RÉAUME, SIMON, *milieu*, Île-à-la-Crosse, wages 500 *livres* (account pages 40d–41). This man was doubtless a member of the fur-trading Réaume family of Montreal and Detroit, but the name Simon is so common in this family that it is impossible to identify him in the baptismal records of Quebec. He became associated with the district of Upper English River, that is, the headwaters of the Beaver River, when it was opened up for the North West Company by Angus Shaw in 1789. In the fall of that year, Shaw wrote from his new fort at Lac d'Orignal, "Simon Reaume lost his way going with letters to Fort des Prairies. He returned yesterday from there and brought me letters from Montreal, from Grand Portage and from Fort des Prairies" (Masson, 1960, I:32). Réaume must be the "old interpreter, good old Simon" who took John McDonald of Garth on his first winter expedition from Lac d'Orignal in the spring of 1792 (ibid., II:14). In 1792–3 Réaume was with Mr Graeme, a North West Company clerk, at Lac d'Orignal, and he and one Coté (perhaps the Louis Coté of the English River Book) were left in charge for the summer (NA MG19, C1–5, 34). Réaume is listed as an interpreter for English River in the North West Company roster of 1797–8 (PAC *Report*, 1939, 56), and as a *commis* at Upper English River in 1799, wages 600 *livres* (Masson, 1960, I:62). The company tried to retire Réaume and send him down to Montreal in 1800; William McGillivray wrote McTavish, Frobisher & Co. from Grand Portage on 19 July of that year: "In the Brigade go down Passengers... old Simon Réaume... Réaume is good for nothing" (NA MG19, B1–1, 145–6). A few days later, however, McGillivray reported that Réaume had not gone down after all: "he got out of the way when the Canoes were going off and is since I understand hired by Mr Forsyth, he owes his descent [that is, his contract required him to work in the canoe down to Montreal before being discharged]... we are well quit of him – he is an old useless man and has been so to my own knowledge for at least 12 years but being an old Servant he was put up with and his being too unreasonable in his demands last Spring was the cause of their bringing him out" (ibid., 152). Nothing has been discovered about Simon Réaume's service for Forsyth and the XY Company.

ROY, PIERRE, *milieu*, perhaps at Île-à-la-Crosse, wages 400 *livres* (account pages 53d–54). His rank is not given, but he was a new man in 1785, with a new man's wages. A Pierre Roy is listed as a canoeman on a trading licence granted to Benjamin Frobisher in 1774 to take four canoes to Grand Portage (Morton Collection, Fur Trade Licences, 314).

SAINT-GERMAIN, PAUL, guide, Athabasca, wages 1000 *livres* (account pages 32d–33; see also Duvalle's account, 15d–16). He is mentioned in the Journal on 5 and 9 April, and 4, 8, and 25 May. In noticing his death in 1804, Peter Fidler said of this North West Company employee that he had "been their principal Guide into the Athapescow Country ever since its first establishment," gave his age at death as sixty-five or sixty-six, and stated that he had been nearly forty years in that country (HBCA B.39/a/3, 12, 29 January 1804; and B.39/a/5ᵇ, 16, same date; these are two versions of the same entry). These ages place Saint-Germain's birth in about 1737, but his baptism has not been found in indexes provided by Charbonneau and Légaré (1980–5) to the baptismal registers of New France. While his career in the fur trade probably extended over more than forty years, the first probable mention so far located is in 1777, when he wintered at Beaver Lake on the communication between Cumberland House and the Churchill River (Rich, 1951, 220; Rich identified this Saint-Germain with Venant Saint-Germain, another North West Company employee and associate, but in the light of later events it seems more reasonable to identify him with Paul, as was done by Tyrrell, 1968a, 392). The following season Saint-Germain and Louis Primot took six canoes to the upper Churchill River, "nigh hand to the A,tho,pus,kow, Country where Primo wintered two Years ago. They are in the employ of Mr Frobisher and Partners" (Rich, 1951, 257), although Saint-Germain himself – if it was still the same man – seems to have wintered on Namew Lake, near Cumberland House, in 1778–9 (ibid., 287–8). These activities, which were part of the Frobishers' expansion of the fur trade onto the Churchill and beyond, towards Athabasca itself, would probably have led to the responsible position which Paul Saint-Germain occupies in the English River Book in 1785–6, as guide to the Athabasca brigade. It is in this context that he is mentioned in Alexander Mackenzie's letters (Lamb, 1970, 425, 427, 431, 441–2, though Lamb also identifies him with Venant Saint-Germain). He is said to have built a trading house for the Crees, dependent on the main Athabasca fort, on the east side of the Athabasca River not far below the mouth of the Clearwater, before 1790 (Tyrrell, 1968a, 392 n). Saint-Germain figures prominently in James McKenzie's journal at Fort Chipewyan in 1799–1800 (Masson, 1960, II:378, 391, 393–4). When Charles Bellegarde, a former XY Company employee, was hired by the North West Company in Athabasca in 1802, to act as *commis* and interpreter, his contract stipulated that he should receive the same equipment (clothing and goods) as "Paul St. Germain etant le plus ancient Commis et interpret Au Athabasca" (HBCA F.5/1, 47). This entry shows that Saint-Germain was no longer acting as a canoeman by that date. Peter Fidler, in his Nottingham House journal of 1803–4, records that Saint-Germain "called Buffalo head" was the North West Company's master at its trading outpost at Fond du Lac, the eastern end of Lake Athabasca, but fell sick, and died on 16 January 1804 after an illness of two months (HBCA B.39/a/3, 12, and B.39/a/5^b, 16, both under date 29 January 1804). MacGregor (1966, 155) has suggested that Paul Saint-Germain was the ancestor of the Saint-Germains of Athabasca. He certainly had a Métis daughter, whom Wentzel, on her father's instructions, tried to get from her mother, a Peace River Indian, in August 1800 (NA MG19, C1–15, 17–18). In the spring of 1804, another daughter was offered as a wife to an XY Company hunter by James McKenzie, the North West Company's master at Fort Chipewyan, in an attempt to hire him away from the opposition (HBCA B.39/a/5^b, 23, 5 May 1804). Men named Saint-Germain who were on the Athabasca books of the North West Company and Hudson's Bay Company in the early nineteenth century may well have been sons and grandsons of Paul Saint-Germain.

SAINT-PIERRE, JEAN-BAPTISTE, *milieu*, Île-à-la-Crosse, wages 300 *livres* (account pages 41d–42). A new man in 1785. There was a voyageur of this name at Rat River in 1805 (Masson, 1960, 1:405).

SCAVOYARD, JEAN-BAPTISTE, *milieu*, Athabasca, wages 500 *livres* (account pages 46d–47). He engaged on 7 April 1786 to serve three years at Great Slave Lake (Journal; he is also mentioned on 5 April). He may have been one of the five voyageurs who were drowned at the Rapids of the Drowned, in Slave River, in the fall of 1786 (see page xxxvii).

SMALL, PATRICK, North West Company partner in charge of English River proper in 1785 with his headquarters probably at Île-à-la-

Crosse. He is mentioned in the Journal at 6 May, and in the accounts of Ledoux (pages 21d–22), Brousseau (26d–27), Monette (31d–32) and Rapin (44d–45). W.S. Wallace's biographical note, though undocumented as usual, provides the basic facts about his life (Wallace, 1934, 498–9).

THESSON, JEAN-BAPTISTE, *milieu*, Athabasca, wages 350 *livres* (account pages 27d–28). Not mentioned in the Journal under this name; no further information.

TOURANGEAU, ANTOINE, *commis*, Île-à-la-Crosse, wages 800 *livres* (account pages 38d–39; de Raimond's account, 49d–50, gives Tourangeau's first name). One of the inventories of goods in the English River Book is an "Accot of Goods sent by Tourengeaux to Trade with the Indians between L'Isle a la Crosse & the River au Rapid – May 1786" (page 63d). To judge from later practice, Tourangeau was sent ahead of the New Concern's brigade to trade any furs or provisions which he could find along the upper Churchill, so that the New Concern would not get them on their way out. Tourangeau is mentioned by Alexander Mackenzie as in English River in August 1787 (Lamb, 1970, 425). He was in charge of the outpost at Lac Poule d'Eau (now Waterhen Lake, Alberta) in 1792–3; by April he had traded about eighteen packs of furs. He was left in charge of Île-à-la-Crosse post for the summer of 1793 (NA MG19, C1–5, 4, 16–17, 25, 42). In 1797–8, Antoine Touranjeau was listed as an interpreter in English River with one year to serve on his contract (PAC *Report*, 1939, 56). He is in the 1799 roster of clerks, with a salary of 1000 *livres* (Masson, 1960, 1:60), but not in the lists of North West Company employees for 1805 or 1806, and probably had retired. Dr Mary Black-Rogers has discovered that Antoine Tourangeau's daughter Angélique was married to Jacques Hamelin in the northwest by 1796: they had three children, the eldest five years and one month old when the couple was married by a priest at Repentigny on 15 February 1802. Angélique's mother was called Marie Caribou, a "sauvagesse," and Angélique herself was described as "sauvagesse native de la Rivière Rouge pays d'en haut" (Catholic register of Repentigny). She was probably born in the early 1780s, and the fact that she was called a native of Red River may mean that Antoine Tourangeau was stationed in the Red River district before he went to English River. Dr Black-Rogers has also pointed out to me that Jean-Baptiste Tourangeau, who started the Métis family of that name in Athabasca, was likely the son of Antoine.

TRANCHEMONTAGNE, —, apparently a Grand Portage guide, mentioned in the account of Bonavan Parisien (page 39d). An Alexis Tranchemontagne was engaged by the Frobishers on 12 February 1784 to go to Grand Portage (APQ *Rapport*, 1946–7, 330). John Gregory reported to Simon McTavish in November 1791: "Tranchemontagne is Engaged to us, at Which Mr. A. Todd was Much Displeased, I Told Him it was Only returning what He Lent Me last year with Blanchard" (HBCA F.3/1, 30).

VANDRIEL, J., is mentioned in François Monette's account as the recipient of a payment of 300 *livres*, by way of "P Small's dft" (page 31d). It is likely that this man is the same as the "Mr Vandreil" who is mentioned several times in Alexander Mackenzie's letters to his cousin Roderick. John Cornelius Vandriel was a native of London, who was baptized at the Independent Church, New Broad Street, on 29 August 1762; the names of his parents are not given in the register (International Genealogical Index, London section). From Mackenzie's references, it appears that Vandriel was a North West Company clerk who was stationed at Île-à-la-Crosse in 1788–9 and transferred to Athabasca for 1789–90 to replace Charles Boyer, then leaving the country. Vandriel evidently had some knowledge of surveying (perhaps learned from Mackenzie), since Mackenzie expected him to make surveys and take observations on his road out to Grand Portage in the spring of 1790 (Lamb, 1970, 436, 438–43). The original survey of the lower course of Peace River as far as the Old Establishment near the modern Fort Vermilion was performed by Vandriel (Mackenzie, 1801, 124). He is not mentioned in Athabasca records after this; probably he left the North West Company and is the Mr Vandriel who sailed for London from Quebec on the fur ship *Eweretta* in the fall of 1970 (Quebec *Gazette*, 28 October 1790). The subscription list for John Long's *Voyages and Travels of an Indian Interpreter and Trader*, which was published in London in 1791, includes Mr J.C. Vandriel (Long, 1791). Subsequently Vandriel must have returned briefly to Canada, since "Mr Vandereel" sailed aboard the *Nancy* from Quebec for London in October 1792 (Quebec *Gazette*, 1 November 1792). Still interested in the fur trade, he accepted a five-year contract with the Hudson's Bay Company on

20 February 1793, to serve inland, at £50 per year (HBCA A.1/47, 10d–11). Vandriel arrived at York Factory on the ship *Prince of Wales* in the fall of that year (HBCA B.239/a/95, 46, 12 August 1793), and was sent inland at once, spending the winter at South Branch House on the South Saskatchewan River (HBCA B.239/a/95, 46d, 1 September 1793; B.205/a/8, 6d, 18 October 1793). Vandriel remained at the South Branch for the summer of 1794, and was the sole survivor of a massacre of the Hudson's Bay Company's servants there, by a large party of Fall Indians, on 24 June 1794; he saved himself by hiding in a cellar (for references and a synopsis of the incident, see Johnson, 1967, 75–6). Vandriel made his way to Cumberland House and reported what had happened; he returned to York Factory with the canoes bringing the season's returns in August (B.239/a/96, 50d, 11 August 1794). Perhaps unwilling to return inland after his terrifying experience, Vandriel was sent to Churchill (ibid., 58, 19 September 1794; B.42/a/121a, 3, 3 October 1794). A letter from the Governor and Committee, which would not have reached him until September 1795, expressed their sympathy for him and their confidence that he would make himself useful inland from Churchill (HBCA A.5/2, 158). Vandriel remained at Churchill Fort all winter, and on 7 September 1795 he was "sent on board the Ship for England" (B.42/a/121a, 27d). This seems to have ended his fur trade career in western Canada.

VENANCE, —, *milieu* (account pages 33d–34). Placed on the books for the English River district, 1785–6, but no wages are recorded for him, nor are expenses after 16 August 1785, and he may not have reached English River. No further information.

VERTIFEUILLE, JOACHIM, *milieu*, Île-à-la-Crosse, wages 300 *livres* (account pages 39d–40). No further information.

NOTES

The following abbreviations are used in the notes:

ANQ-M   Archives nationales du Quebec, Montreal
APQ   Archives de la Province de Quebec
HBCA   Hudson's Bay Company Archives,
        Provincial Archives of Manitoba
NA   National Archives of Canada
PAC   Public Archives of Canada
PAM   Provincial Archives of Manitoba

INTRODUCTION

1 At least eight pages, probably all blank, have been cut from the book, perhaps as paper was needed for other purposes in 1785–6. When the book was paginated by archivists, the page following 36 was missed, and the present numbering therefore includes pages 36A and 36B. The significance of the notation "R.R.R." on the cover is obscure.

2 Rat River was the name used by the North Westers for the district lying east of the canoe route up the Sturgeon-Weir River to Frog Portage. Malchom Ross, the Hudson's Bay Company servant, passed through the district in the early fall of 1786, met Jurial Baldwin, the Canadian trader, on the Kississing River, and learned from him that his trading house in 1785–6 had been on Kississing Lake: see biography of Jurial Baldwin in appendix B. According to Ross, "these Canadians is been this 3 year about this Tracks... that is one canoe or two only that they send in "(HBCA B.49/a/18, 6 September 1786). This statement would date the beginning of the Canadians' Rat River trade to the season of 1783–4.

3 Douglas, 1929.

4 Since Fleming was assistant editor of the Hudson's Bay Record Society volumes at the time, it is possible that the English River Book was actually considered for publication about 1940. I am indebted to Mrs S.A. Smith for this suggestion.

5 An idea of the scale of the Frobishers' trade can be formed from the Indian trade licences granted to them at this period. In 1769 Dobie and Frobisher sent three canoes to Michilimackinac (U. of Saskatchewan Special Collections, Morton Collection, Fur Trade Licences, 61, 68); and three to Michilimackinac and Grand Portage in 1770 (117). In 1772 Benjamin and Joseph Frobisher sent three canoes to Grand Portage (223), and four in 1774 (314; the 1773 licences are incomplete). A consortium consisting of James McGill, Benjamin Frobisher, and Maurice Blondeau sent twelve canoes to Grand Portage in 1775 (274–5). As Innis noted, this large consolidated shipment in 1775 "appears to mark... the beginning of the Northwest Company" (Innis, 1970, 194).

6 All of our detailed information about the Frobishers' development of the trade on the Churchill River comes from the Hudson's Bay Company journals kept at Cumberland House from 1774 onwards and from other related documents. These have been published up to 1783. Key references in these volumes are: Tyrrell, 1968a, 106–7, 115, 120–2, 130–1, 150, 188–90, 194, 241n; and Rich, 1951, 15–16, 27–30, 36–7, 59–66.

7 Rich, 1951, 29, 59–60. Turnor in 1790 noted the site of the trading house of "Lewis Primo" on Primeau Lake, and Tyrrell, 1968a, 41, 354n, suggested that this was where Primot wintered in 1775–6.

8 Mackenzie, 1801, xii, states definitely that Joseph Frobisher's brother was the first to reach Île-à-la-Crosse. The Cumberland House journal says that "the Elder Forbisher" was in charge of this expedition (Rich, 1951, 66), which should mean Joseph himself, but there is no reason to believe that the Hudson's Bay people knew who was the elder and who the younger brother. Joseph Frobisher went to Montreal with Alexander Henry in 1776 and did not return to the northwest again (Henry, 1969, 335–8; Mackenzie, 1801, xii).

9 For Frobisher's and Primot's movements, see Rich, 1951, 93–4, 117–18, 149, 165–6, 257. During the winter of 1776–7, letters were received on the upper Saskatchewan from the Churchill traders, which had been forwarded overland from Île-à-la-Crosse (ibid., 117–18).

10 Rich, 1951, 94, 119, 217, 220. In 1778–9, Saint-Germain and Primot were said to be in the Frobishers' employ (ibid., 257). It was been assumed that this Saint-Germain was Venant Saint-Germain, but a

likelier candidate is perhaps Paul Saint-Germain, the Athabasca guide who appears in the English River Book (see his biography).

11 Mackenzie, 1801, xii-xiii.

12 Rich, 1951, 235–6.

13 Rich, 1952, 6. Pond wintered in 1778–9 at the Old Establishment, the place where he was in 1785–8 (Mackenzie, 1801, lxxxvii).

14 Rich, 1952, 52.

15 Mackenzie, 1801, xiii; Rich, 1952, 68.

16 Mackenzie, 1801, xvi (which wrongly dates this episode to 1780–1); Davidson, 1967, 41 and note; Wallace, 1954, 21–4; Wagner, 1955, 10–11.

17 HBCA B.49/a/13, 13 and 23 September 1782. Small had traded near Cranberry Portage, in the hinterland of Cumberland House, in 1779–80 (Rich, 1952, 17, 29, 37, 48–9) and had a licence to take goods from Montreal to Detroit, with Simon McTavish as surety, in 1781 (Morton Collection, Fur Trade Licences, 504).

18 Mackenzie, 1801, xvi-xvii, again dates these events one year too early. I follow the dating adopted by Innis, 1930, 98, who also used the evidence of Pond's maps.

19 Mackenzie, 1801, xviii, reports Pond's dissatisfaction. There is much evidence for his presence at Montreal in 1784–5: Innis, 1930, 104–6; Wagner, 1955, 11–15.

20 HBCA B.49/a/15, 11 and 15 September 1784; B.49/a/16, 26 June 1785. While none of these references specifically states that either Small or Montour was going for the Churchill or beyond, it is natural to assume that Small, at least, was assigned to the post he later occupied at Île-à-la-Crosse. Montour was posted to the Saskatchewan in other seasons, but Pond's absence in 1784–5 would have necessitated a replacement, and Montour's association with Small in this season, including his arrival with Small at Cumberland House on 25 June 1785 (weeks after the Saskatchewan brigade would have left for Grand Portage), seems easiest to explain if Montour was Pond's replacement in Athabasca in 1784–5.

21 Innis, 1927, 309–10.

22 Mackenzie, 1801, xviii.

23 One Pierre Belair was hired by Pangman and Ross to go to Fort des Prairies (the Saskatchewan) on 23 September 1784, and one François Barille to go to Rivière des Anglais (the Churchill) on 27 December 1784: APQ *Rapport*, 1946–7, 341.

24 The documents are printed or cited in Innis, 1930, 94–6; Wallace, 1954, 22–3; Wagner, 1955, 12–13 especially n 9; and Davidson, 1967, 41 n 43.

25 Wagner, 1955, 13–14, 80–4.

26 Tyrrell, 1968a, 53–4; Rich, 1951, 202, 205, 211–23.

27 Morton Collection, Fur Trade Licences, 495–6; Wallace, 1934, 66.

28 Morton Collection, Fur Trade Licences, 499–500.

29 HBCA B.22/a/1, 18 September 1793, locates Ross's fort of 1780 on the Assiniboine. The so-called diary of Donald Mackay, who acted as a clerk for Ross on the Assiniboine in 1780–1, records aspects of this season (HBCA copy no. 626). Mackay also served Ross in 1779–80 but gives no details.

30 HBCA B.49/a/16, 2 September 1785.

31 Ibid., 20 September 1785.

32 Roderick McKenzie's Reminiscences, in Masson, 1960, I:11. Leroux was certainly employed by the New Concern in 1785–6, but McKenzie does not give his station.

33 APQ *Rapport*, 1946–7, 341, 344.

34 The site, which is thought to have been washed away, is discussed by Parker, 1976, 38.

35 See Journal, 4d. The Hudson's Bay Company did not send an expedition into English River and Athabasca until 1790, and did not come to trade to English River until 1799, and to Athabasca until 1803. One reason was the shortage of manpower available to them, compared to the much larger North West Company. Also important was the reluctance of William Tomison, the Hudson's Bay Company's chief inland from York Factory, to support any new venture that would drain resources from the Saskatchewan River. See Rich, 1959, 140–6, and Tyrrell, 1968a, 598–600.

36 See a copy of this map in Wagner, 1955, Map Number Three. Another version is the Ezra Stiles copy, dated 1790, reproduced by Davidson, 1967, 42.

37 Tyrrell, 1968a, 440n. The site of "Grants Old House" was used for outposts from Fort Chipewyan, "in case any Inds passes that way," by the North West Company and the XY Company in 1804–5, the last season that they opposed one another (HBCA B.39/a/5b, 42d, 22 November 1804), and the fishery there supported twenty-one men during the fall of 1821 (HBCA B.39/a/20, 17, 7 October 1821).

38 Tyrrell, 1968a, 401–2. Peace River was first reached by Canadian traders in 1786 (Mackenzie, 1801, 146), and their first settlement was probably the so-called Old Establishment, near Fort Vermilion (ibid., 124, 129).

39 This dependent fort, passed by Philip Turnor and his party on 23 June 1791 and said to be abandoned, was described by him as follows: "an

old Canadian House on East side which was left when they built the one at the mouth of the Pillicon River [the Clearwater] it was a Winter trading House for the Southern Indians [Crees] and dependent on the Athapescow Lake House" (Tyrrell, 1968a, 392). Peter Fidler, who was with Turnor, recorded that the house had been established by "St. Germain or Buffalo Head" (ibid., 392 n), that is, by the North West Company's Athabasca guide, Paul Saint-Germain. The post which replaced it was built by Alexander McLeod for the company in 1787 or 1788 (ibid., 389 and n).

40 Mackenzie, 1801, 14 n.

41 Lamb, 1970, 424.

42 See the inventory in the English River Book of "Sundries sent in 2 Canoes to Arabasca the 31st May 1786 – to be delivered Mr Pond by A Derrie" (pages 117–19). Many of the Athabasca men's accounts list "sundries" or particular articles sold to them at Île-à-la-Crosse on 1 June 1786, which suggests that the Athabasca men arrived there on that date.

43 See account of goods left in charge of Mr Lesieur, Île-à-la-Crosse, dated 4 June 1786, pages 120–2.

44 HBCA B.49/a/17.

45 Mackenzie, 1801, 5. Philip Turnor gives the story, but without mentioning Grant by name; Tyrrell, 1968a, 406.

46 Mackenzie, 1801, 8 (the date 1785 is corrected to 1786 on the errata page); Tyrrell, 1968a, 517–19 and n. The last reference, which is from Peter Fidler's journal, states: "The Canadians were compelled to abandon these Houses they could not catch any fish which is the only thing to depend upon amongst the Jepewyans One man was eaten by 2 others here thro' necessity."

47 Bigsby, 1969, I:117; quoted, from the original edition, by Wagner, 1955, 42.

48 Tyrrell, 1968a, 417 and n.

49 Masson, 1960, I:18–19.

50 For reproductions of this map, see note 36. Isaac Ogden's letter to his father, recounting his talk with Peter Pond in 1789, says that Pond had explored the Mackenzie River some seventy miles from its outlet from Great Slave Lake, as far as the "Falls," whose size Alexander Mackenzie later found to be greatly exaggerated: Wagner, 1955, 89–90; Mackenzie, 1801, 28–30.

51 Wagner, 1955, 96.

52 APQ Rapport, 1943–4, 366.

53 HBCA F.3/1, 2, 3, 5–8, 10–15.

54 Quoted by Wagner, 1955, 44.

55 HBCA F.4/32, page 769; B.239/g/1, 73; B.239/g/2, 89; B.39/a/20, 2d, 32d, 36, 41, 42d.

56 Although the canoes from the less remote posts had to go to Grand Portage to deliver their furs and get their new ladings of goods, this was impossible for the Athabasca brigades if they were to return to the north safely before freeze-up. For Athabasca alone, then, a depot was established at Lac La Pluie, which saved twenty-five to thirty days on the round trip. The idea of using Lac La Pluie for this purpose may have been proposed by Peter Pond.

57 Wallace, 1934, 329.

58 In the fall of 1820 George Simpson noted the discontent of the North West Company's brigade men, because the Lac La Pluie shop had not been able to provide "their full supplies of necessaries" (Rich, 1938, 25).

59 In the accounts of Henry Caesar and Charles Papan, both Athabasca men, tobacco was charged at a rate of 30 *livres* per fathom; in all the other accounts, the rate at Île-à-la-Crosse was 20 *livres* per fathom.

60 The suggested interpretation of the tobacco "overcharges" would imply a 50 per cent advance of Athabasca prices over those at Île-à-la-Crosse, and 225 per cent over those at Lac La Pluie. Philip Turnor in 1792 listed a number of prices, in terms of beaver skins, for Peace River, Great Slave Lake, and Athabasca, in which the prices at the first two places were the same, and were mostly 20 to 50 per cent greater than those at Athabasca (Tyrrell, 1968a, 451). The 1803 North West Company minutes include a schedule of surcharges on trade goods sent to the different departments – the surcharges varied with the class of goods, but an average assortment cost 87 per cent more at Lac La Pluie, 113 per cent more at English River, and 130 per cent more anywhere in Athabasca, relative to Fort William prices (Wallace, 1934, 197).

61 Various North West Company documents give data which show that 12 *livres* were still taken as equal to £1 Halifax currency as late as 1821; see calculations of the costs of clerks' equipments, at £20 each, in *livres* or "G.P. Currency," in Masson, 1960, 1: 61–6; and HBCA F.4/32, 669, 671, 759, for examples of clerks whose wages are expressed both in Halifax currency and in *livres*. Other accounts in the latter document give the equivalent in *livres* of clerks' wages which were originally expressed in pounds sterling (pages 647, 697, 707, 711). Those accounts show that 20 *livres* were taken as equal to £1 sterling. Since all these accounts were simply paper transactions, and the *livre* no longer existed except as an accounting currency for the fur trade, the rates of

exchange between the different currencies might remain constant indefinitely.

62 There are a few instances of the same practice in the North West Company's ledger of men's accounts for 1811–21 (HBCA F.4/32), but they are rare. It is possible that Pond was more complaisant than usual in 1786, in view of the danger that his best men might hire with Ross and the New Concern if he drove too hard a bargain.

63 Of the other seven, three were new men (Bleau, Labrêche, and Venance) who had come up from Montreal, were placed on the English River books, but seem not to have proceeded beyond Lac La Pluie; two (Ainsse and LePin) seem to have retired; one (Calvé) "wint^d at Fort des Prairies," on the Saskatchewan; and one (Lafrance) had died during the summer of 1785. All these details come from the individual men's accounts.

64 The word *commis* originally was just the French equivalent of clerk. By the 1790s, there seems to have been some distinction between the two terms, in that some men who had the title *commis* cannot have been qualified to carry out the bookkeeping duties expected of clerks more recently hired. While the *commis* conducted the actual trade, a writer or petty accountant would be provided him to ensure the keeping of detailed records. By the early 1800s the company was retiring its older *commis* and putting the trade entirely in the hands of English-speaking clerks who had been trained in accounting and the keeping of journals and books. Hudson's Bay Company servants used the term "half-gentlemen," perhaps not entirely contemptuously, in referring to the North West Company *commis*, and the term "postmaster" was used for this sort of employee after the 1821 union of the two companies.

65 This list is in Wallace, 1934, 219–21.

66 The twelve English River Book voyageurs who seem to appear in HBCA F.4/32, are Aubuchon, Babeu, Brousseau, Cardinal, Cartier, Constantineau, Lafleur, Ignace Lavallé, Letendre, Maranda, Nasplette, and Parisien; some identifications may be made with more confidence than others. The five who retired in 1822, after the coalition, were Babeu, Constantineau, Lafleur, Lavallé, and Letendre.

THE JOURNAL

1 Arabasca is Peter Pond's original orthography, as seen on his maps. Although the modern spelling Athabasca soon superseded it (thanks probably to Alexander Mackenzie; Philip Turnor used *Athapiscow* and *Athapescow*), the older spelling is occasionally seen as late as the 1820s.

2 Bigg Chief: see appendix A.

3 A pack was about ninety pounds – the weight was standardized since it had to be portaged repeatedly. This pack, if all in full-size beaver pelts, would contain about sixty to seventy skins.

4 Alexis Derry, a *commis* or clerk: see appendix B.

5 Great Slave Lake.

6 The custom of sending a "young man" to a post for tobacco before coming in to trade was usual in the fur country.

7 The Tittons: see appendix A.

8 The Athapaskan Indians occupying the Peace River valley; see Jenness, 1977, 382–4.

9 Little Lake Arabasca is not certainly identified, but it may have been the lake immediately west of Lake Athabasca now called Lake Claire. The name Clear Lake was in use by 1803 (HBCA B.39/a/2, 45).

10 The Beaver River Indians were Crees, living in the valley of the Beaver River, which falls into the Churchill at Île-à-la-Crosse.

11 Chipewyans, the principal Athapaskan tribe, caribou hunters from the edge of the Barrens (Jenness, 1977, 385–8).

12 It was the custom for trading Indians to be given goods on credit in the fall for which the trader expected payment in the spring. In the Journal a distinction is made between paying credits and "trading" furs or provisions. "Trading" occurred only if the fall debts had been paid and furs or provisions were left over.

13 This drinking bout or *boisson* was typical of certain occasions, such as when the trader arrived in the fall with the new goods, or when the major trading session, in the spring, was under way. Although many traders' journals note the violence sometimes associated with a *boisson*, it was a well-established event, and the traders felt that they could not dispense with it.

14 Because of the traders' difficulty in living off the land, major trade commodities were fresh ("green") and dried meat, which was consumed at the post. Later, the traders moved to become more independent of casual supplies of provisions by hiring fort hunters on contracts and storing large numbers of frozen carcasses.

15 Clerk Charles Boyer or Boyé: see appendix B.

16 L'homme de Castor, "the man of the beaver," see appendix A. The Journal makes no attempt to write down the actual name of any Indian in his own language, but some names used may be translations of actual Indian names.

17 The two Cadiens were Joseph Landry and Charles Doucette: see appendix B.

18 Dominique Ledoux.

19 Jean-Baptiste Laprise.

20 Joseph Perrault.

21 François Laviolette.

22 Janvier Mayotte.

23 Louis Brousseau.

24 François Faniant.

25 Charles Doucette.

26 Probably Claude Deveau. Pierre Duvalle, the other similar name in the Account Book, appears to have been known in the Journal as *Pierish*: see appendix B.

27 Rivière au Hallier may have something to do with the French word *hallier*, which can mean a thicket, or (perhaps by extension) an animal snare (Ledésert and Ledésert, 1972, H:3). The river was evidently about five days' walk from the fort, since the party did not return until 13 April. The name occurs as Rivière au Harrier in the 1821–2 Fort Chipewyan journal in a context which suggests that it was approached from the lower part of the Athabasca River (HBCA B.39/a/20, 32, 34d). Probably it was one of the rivers which flows out of Birch Mountain, west of Athabasca River, but all of these except the largest, Birch River (already called Bark River by Fidler in 1804: B.39/a/5^b, 37, 25 September 1804), seem to have been renamed since the fur trade days.

28 The Shining Rock (see appendix A) is referred to again on 11 April by the French equivalent, *la roche qui reluit*.

29 A beaver robe consisted of as many as eight skins stitched together and was the most desirable form of beaver to the trader because wearing the fur had taken off the guard hairs. The Beaver Indian who had traded it while drunk was now feeling the cold, not surprising in northern Alberta in mid-April. Credit was rarely given in the spring.

30 A *capot*, a common trading item, was a kind of cloth cloak.

31 Tobacco, in small quantities, would have been given to the Indian, and this man, probably left with nothing to trade, took some in the hope that he could use it to buy a robe.

32 A poignard, or a dirk or dagger. The situation having been mishandled cost Pond more than it would have at first. Probably Pond was anxious to placate the Indian only because of John Ross's opposition in Athabasca.

33 These are not packs, which required pressing, but only a temporary way of consolidating the furs.

34 Canoe *maîtres*. This is the first of several entries relating to Boyer's canoe-making activities. Four new canoes were built, the wood of two others was reused (see entry of 6 April), and two other "old" canoes

were also used to make up the eight needed for the outward brigade. The canoe *maîtres* were long timbers (Williams, 1973, 22 n), and must therefore have been the gunwales, the only long wooden pieces in a birchbark canoe (Adney and Chapelle, 1983, 31, 37–9). This is the meaning given by Avis (1967, 457). For further discussion of the word *maître*, see Inventories note 44.

35 Lac du Brochet (pike or jackfish lake) is noted by Philip Turnor in 1791 (Tyrrell, 1968a, 395), and is frequently mentioned in George Simpson's Fort Wedderburn journal of 1820–1 (Rich, 1938, 318). The most prominent lake in the Athabasca delta and called Richardson Lake on the topographical maps, is still known locally as Jackfish Lake. It is an important fishery for some spawning runs. I am indebted to Dr Patricia A. McCormack for this information.

36 A train of meat was a sled laden with meat to be traded.

37 Jean-Baptiste Scavoyard.

38 Paul Saint-Germain, the Athabasca guide.

39 The bark was for making and mending canoes. The mountain must be the Birch Mountains, on the west side of the Athabasca River, west and south of the fort.

40 Given the evidence that *maître* sometimes meant a long piece of wood used to control something or hold it in place (see note 34), *maître de médecine* might be the stem of a ceremonial pipe, whose importance is shown by the fact that Pond forbade Boyer to make one of his own. An apparent synonym is *manetre de paix*; see note 51.

41 *Gabarit* means mould or template, especially as used in shipbuilding; *lisse* is the handrail of a ship's bulwark, and has other meanings, all referring to longitudinal structures in a ship (Ledésert and Ledésert, 1972, G:1, L:21). Avis (1967, 431) quotes a definition of *lisses* as the ribs of a birchbark canoe. Ribs were not longitudinal pieces, however, and it is unlikely that the journalist would have remarked on the completion of two ribs, since many more would have been required for even one canoe. In canoe building, it seems likely that the *gabarit* was what is called in English the building frame, while the *lisse* would be the gunwale frame. See Adney and Chapelle, 1983, 36 ff, for a detailed account of the construction of a birchbark canoe.

42 Joseph Laverdure.

43 Pierre Marcille.

44 The "Lack" in this case is probably Lake Athabasca, and the two canoes had probably been used to settle the outpost on the north shore of the lake (see introduction, page xix).

45 La Bonne does not appear in the Account Book under this name, and he has not been identified. For possibilities see the entry La Bonne in appendix B. This man and his five companions were probably those

assigned to the Lake Athabasca outpost during the winter. They were now returning to the main post to assist with the spring trade and to prepare for the voyage out to Lac La Pluie.

46 This new arrival must be Joseph Landrieffe (see appendix B), rather than Joseph Landry *dit* Cadien, since the latter was already at the fort on 3 April, when he was hired for Great Slave Lake. Landrieffe himself was hired for the same place on 7 April.

47 François Bouché.

48 Pierre Dumas.

49 The Boudar: see appendix A.

50 *Above* means from the south, up the valley of the River Athabaca, while *below* means from the north, the direction of Lake Athabasca.

51 *Manetre de Paix* appears from the context to be a synonym for *Maître de medicine* (see note 40); taking the two expressions together, one might suggest the stem of a ceremonial pipe. If *manetre* is not a misspelling of *maître* it could be *manette*, "petit levier, poignée ou clef se manoeuvrant à la main pour faire agir un mécanisme" (Bélisle, 1954, 741).

52 Louis Brisbois.

53 Passpartout is Joseph Nasplette, *dit* Pass-par-tout.

54 Like the men hired to winter at Great Slave Lake on 3 April, these were intended to staff the new post to be built on the lake in summer 1786: see introduction, page xix.

55 River la paix is Peace River, which was also to be settled in the summer of 1786. "Old Joseph" was either Joseph Duchain or Joseph Maranda, the two Josephs who were at Athabasca and are not mentioned in the Journal by their proper names (see appendix B).

56 Food was not cooked in common for the men, but instead they were issued rations according to what was available in the fort at the time.

57 Carcajeau, i.e., carcajou, a wolverine: see appendix A.

58 Chantair: see appendix A.

59 Henry Caesar.

60 Jean-Baptiste Languedocque.

61 La Grain and L'Orignal were fort hunters: see appendix A.

62 Pierre Bellanger.

63 Grand Portage is probably not meant, as the Athabasca brigade actually went only as far as Lac La Pluie on their journey out: see introduction, page xxv. Perhaps Pond had in mind an arrangement by which the Athabasca summer men would meet incoming canoes at Portage La Loche.

64 The English Chief was the best-known trading Chipewyan: see appendix A.

65 This seems to show that Alexis Derry spent part of the winter at an outpost, where the Old Chief was an important customer.

66 The Chiefe Cancre: see appendix A.

67 Grand Piccotte: see appendix A.

68 It was strongly suspected that these Indians were delaying their visit to the fort in the hope of meeting John Ross, who might give them a better price. The claim to have few furs may have been intended to discourage Pond from trying to interfere with this trade.

69 This must be Joseph Guyette d'Yamaska, whose account shows that he was paid 200 *livres* for making a trip to Athabasca during the winter.

70 Earlier referred to as the Shining Rock; see appendix A.

71 *Orignal* or moose was another trading item.

72 The Gendre was another fort hunter; see appendix A.

73 Pierish is not in the accounts under this name, but may be Pierre Duvalle: see Pierish in appendix B.

74 Although the Gendre had killed the moose and sold it to the traders, it was not his responsibility to bring it to the fort himself.

75 Duvaut and Duveau apparently are the same person.

76 This party had left the fort on 3 April.

77 Jean-Baptiste Lafleur.

78 Charles Papan (the other Papan in the Account Book, Joseph, was at Île-à-la-Crosse).

79 The little Orignal was another casual hunter: see appendix A.

80 Philippe Bruillette.

81 Bras Cassé: see appendix A.

82 The Portage de Pin was on the Clearwater River: see entry of 20 May, and note 130.

83 *Écore*, "rive escarpée d'une rivière" (Bergeron, 1980, 196). This was a point where the banks of the Athabasca River were higher, so that there was no danger of flooding as at the fort.

84 The Lac du Poisson Blanc, or Whitefish Lake, was evidently no more than half a day's walk from the fort, and was probably one of the small lakes just east of it, such as Blanche Lake, Limon Lake, or Dagmar Lake. Although ice fishing was perfectly practicable in winter, there was no point in sending men to fish for a living at a lake which was about to break up, since thawing ice was dangerous and could carry away the nets. Once the lake was clear, fishing would be done from canoes.

85 Peccant: see appendix A.

86 "Clothing" a chief was an important ceremony when an influential trading Indian appeared, Special "chief's coats," a sort of uniform, were devised for this purpose.

87 During the *boisson* or drinking bout, the traders had to remain awake day and night, selling liquor for furs as the Indians required.

88 This is the only mention in the Journal of John Ross, the opposition trader for the New Concern. This reference does not show where Ross was except that his fort was probably not nearby. In 1828 Archibald McDonald noted the site of "the old fort of Mr. Ross" on the right bank of the Athabasca River almost opposite the mouth of the River Embarras, several miles below Pond's fort (McLeod, 1971, 11). Except for Samuel Hearne's historic third journey across the Barren Lands in 1770–2, the Hudson's Bay Company servants had never approached the Athabasca country. Indians from that region had been accustomed to go down to Churchill with their furs before Peter Pond came among them, and the Hudson's Bay Company had planned for some time to send an outfit to Athabasca. Ross's bold lie would not have seemed implausible. For The Hand, a trading Indian, see appendix A.

89 Joseph Preux.

90 Probably *collars*, as a portable part of the chief's ceremonial clothing.

91 François Jolybois.

92 Ambroise Lalonde.

93 Both François Bouché and Jean-Marie Bouché were at Athabasca; this was probably François Bouché, the *milieu* since his companion, Larivière, was a *devant* and Jean-Marie, another *devant*, would have been in charge of another canoe.

94 Simon Martin.

95 Jean-Baptiste Brunosh.

96 Weighing the packs was critical because of the repeated portaging. The weight of each was normally ninety ponds; as emerges presently, at this post, in this season, eighty-eight was the standard.

97 Joseph Derry, *gouvernail*.

98 Making the packs required pressing the furs to reduce the bulk from trapped air. Although a fur press is not mentioned in the Journal it would have been a substantial device, perhaps employing a lever, or, as later, a threaded screw and a capstan.

99 Canoes were assembled in "beds" scooped out of the ground, which supported the woodwork and the birch bark until the sewing was complete, and the ribs inserted (see Adney and Chapelle, 1983, 36ff).

100 Augustin Piccott.

101 Presumably the Joseph Guyette whose account appears in the English River Book on pages 33d–34, since the other Joseph Guyette is called d'Yamaska.

102 That is, finished.

103 These furs would have been kept separate, since they were part of the previous year's outfit. This entry shows that Boyer had spent the summer of 1785 in charge of Athabasca Fort, rather than going out to

Lac La Pluie; thus, he also spent the winter of 1784–5 at the fort. Summer furs were less valuable than furs trapped in winter, although any furs obtained after the departure of the canoes in May would also have been included.

104 Alexander Mackenzie wrote in 1792: "In the fall of the year 1787, when I first arrived at Athabasca, Mr. Pond was settled on the banks of the Elk River [the Athabasca River], where he remained for three years, and had formed as fine a kitchen garden as I ever saw in Canada" (Mackenzie, 1801, 129).

105 *Taureaux* of pemmican. A *taureau* was a buffalo skin bag, into which dried, pounded buffalo meat was crammed. Molten fat was then poured in to fill the bag, and the mixture was pemmican. The word *taureau* was also used in the west for the buffalo itself. It will have been noted that few of the animals killed at the Athabasca Fort in 1786 were buffalo (most were moose, a much leaner meat), and it is possible that the pemmican made there was that described by Mackenzie as "Fish dried in the sun, and afterwards pounded for the convenience of carriage" (Mackenzie, 1801, 14 n).

106 Quisson, his given name is unknown, was a *gouvernail*.

107 Because of the short travelling season, it was necessary to get the brigade under way as early as possible, so that it could get to Lac La Pluie and return before freeze-up in the fall.

108 Gum, obtained from pine trees, was used to seal the seams in the canoes, and was taken with the brigade to make repairs, which were frequently needed. This entry is the only specific mention in the Journal of women, some of whom would have been the wives of voyageurs.

109 François Piché.

110 Jean-Baptiste Rapin.

111 The canoes were named for the *devants* who guided them.

112 The island is not identified but was perhaps the low land lying between branches of the Athabasca River delta.

113 Of these men, Saint-Germain was the guide; Martin, Larivière, Jean-Marie Bouché and Caesar were *devants*; Piccott's rank is not specified, but the fact that he was entrusted with command of a canoe shows that he was an experienced man.

114 The Hand, a trading Indian, see entry of 11 May and appendix A.

115 The Portage La Loche or Methy Portage, twelve and a half miles long; for a recent account see Epp and Jones, 1969. It was probably the longest portage in regular use by the fur traders anywhere in the northwest, and the only practicable entry for canoes into Athabasca. What seems to be the earliest surviving use of the name Portage La Loche is in the Journal for 21 May.

116 The *devant* for this canoe was Pierre Duvalle, if he may be identified as the "Pierish" of the Journal.

117 The present Point Brulé, doubtless named because it had been burned over by a fire shortly before it was named. The "league" was a voyageur's measure of distance, supposed to have equalled a bit more than two miles.

118 What may be a reference to this incident with the gun is in the account of Joseph Preux, who was shown as owing Cuthbert Grant 125 livres "for a Gun." Since Preux was the *devant* in a different canoe, he cannot have caused the accident, but he may have owed "Pierish" for something and assumed responsibility. It would have been unlike the North West Company to excuse a man's carelessness which led to the loss of their property, but the gun may have been Grant's own.

119 Pierre à Calumet, the "pipe stone," a well-known place on the Athabasca River, referred to in most of the standard itineraries.

120 The Hand is the Indian whose young men had been sent to the fort with furs.

121 Since the total packs of furs to be taken out in the brigade was 162 (160 packs completed on 6 May, plus two more pressed on the 8th), and the standard lading for a north canoe was about 22 packs, the journalist's canoe might have had a little room for loose furs. The brigade was not carrying trade goods, and so it was necessary to pay the Hand with a billet or credit note, payable at the Athabasca Fort.

122 *Bres* is unrecognizable as French. Is it the Scotch "braes"?

123 *Sallin* is Canadian French *saline*, a salt spring (Bergeron, 1980, 442). The place is marked by Saline Lake, in the Athabasca River valley just east of the river channel.

124 The "little river" is the Clearwater, referred to by George Simpson in 1820 as "Little Athabasca River" (Rich, 1938, 38), and by Malcolm McLeod, editor of Archibald McDonald's journal of Simpson's voyage of 1828, as "La Petite Rivière Râbasca" (McLeod, 1971, 64).

125 Rivière au Pembina is this case is the Christina River, the only large tributary of the Clearwater. George Simpson (Rich, 1938, 327, 344) and Archibald McDonald (McLeod, 1971, 10) both call it Pembina River. Philip Turnor, who may have been translating an Indian name, called it Red Willow River (Tyrrell, 1968a, 460).

126 The rapid is a series of rapids and small waterfalls, extending over about four miles of the Clearwater. Simpson, descending the river, noted three unloading places in the order *Décharge la grosse Roche* (a *décharge* was a place where the goods were portaged, but the vessel itself was taken down by water; in ascending the river, of course, the canoe would also have to be carried), *Portage la Bon*, and *Cascades* (Rich, 1938, 38). McDonald mentions only *La Bonne Rapide* (McLeod, 1971, 10).

127 The *Cascades* was the first part of the rapid (see note 126).

128 The portage must be the same as the Portage la Bon of Simpson (note 126).

129 More frequently Portage de Pin: so called by Simpson (Rich, 1938, 37) and McDonald (McLeod, 1971, 10).

130 The Journal does not specifically mention the last obstacle on the Clearwater before Portage La Loche, the Terre Blanche (Rich, 1938, 38) or Mud Portage (McLeod, 1971, 10).

131 *Biche*, the wapiti or American elk.

132 Philip Turnor, who had to find the north end of Portage La Loche without a guide, having only general directions, passed it by at first. Leaving the Clearwater channel, the canoes passed through a grassy swamp for about a mile to "a peice of fine meadow," where the landing was (Tyrrell, 1968a, 466).

133 Apart from the length of the Portage La Loche, the only difficult part was at the north end. "Within a mile of the termination of the Portage," says Mackenzie, "is a very steep precipice, whose ascent and descent appears to be equally impraticable in any way, as it consists of a succession of eight hills, some of which are almost perpendicular" (Mackenzie, 1801, lxxxv). Turnor's more detailed account is less dramatic, but also notes the dangers (Tyrrell, 1968a, 466–7).

134 See the entry of 9 May. Arrangements had been made for Patrick Small, in charge at Île-à-la-Crosse, to send two canoe loads of trading goods to Athabasca as early as possible, and it had been calculated that these goods would reach the south end of Portage La Loche before the Athabasca brigade was finished carrying over it. Accordingly, two canoes were to be left by the brigade on the north end of the portage, which could be used by the men going to Athabasca, thus avoiding the carrying of two canoes over the portage. As emerges later, the Île-à-la-Crosse men did not make their rendezvous, and the Athabasca brigade had to return over the portage to bring the two canoes after all.

135 The "lack" is Lac La Loche, the first lake encountered on the south side of the portage. This lake, which is near the watershed between the Clearwater and the Churchill drainage, is often full of ice when the fast-moving rivers are clear.

136 The "little lack," now called Rendezvous Lake on the maps, provided "a trifling respite to the labour of carrying" (Mackenzie, 1801, lxxxv).

137 This shrine is not otherwise mentioned, and the identity of Jos Gray is unknown.

138 The Grand Maskege was a large tract of swamp, to one side of the portage trail, slightly more than half way across the portage (see Epp and Jones, 1969).

139 Two men, Joseph Landry *dit* Cadien, and François Bouché, are specifically credited in their accounts with payments of 100 *livres* for carrying canoes "in the Great Portage." For the other six men, the payments must have been included in their general credits. Normally a canoe would be portaged by two men, the *devant* and the *gouvernail*, and the trip would have taken about five days, keeping pace with the carriers of the canoe's lading. By sending four men for each canoe, and paying a large premium (between 10 and 20 per cent of the year's wages), Grant got the canoes over Portage La Loche is less than twenty-four hours. Probably the men marched all night.

140 From the south end of the Portage La Loche the route passed through a short creek into Lac La Loche, and then across it to Rivière La Loche, its outlet.

141 Lac du Boeuf or Buffalo Lake, now Peter Pond Lake.

142 The usual canoe route was apparently on the east side of the lake and involved a long *traverse* or crossing of open water. Both Simpson and McDonald (McLeod, 1971, 9) mention this traverse, and Simpson says of Buffalo Lake: "This is a very stormy Lake being much exposed by its high situation, and Canoes are frequently wind bound several days" (Rich, 1938, 35).

143 The little *détroit* is the present Buffalo Narrows, a strait passage between Peter Pond Lake and Churchill Lake, the Lac Claire of the voyageurs.

144 Rivière Creuse of Mackenzie (Mackenzie, 1801, lxxxiv). One of the goods inventories in the English River Book is headed "Accot of Sundries sent in 2 Canoes to Arabasca the 31st May 1786 – to be deliverd Mr Pond by A. Derrie." Evidently the men from Île-à-la-Crosse, who had set off much later than intended, met the Athabasca brigade on Lac Claire shortly after the last entry in the Journal was completed. There was perhaps some exchange of men in the canoes, and Alexis Derry with the goods returned to Athabasca, while the main brigade, with the journalist, proceeded to Île-à-la-Crosse which they probably reached on 1 June.

INVENTORIES

1 The Oxford English Dictionary defines *strouds* as blankets made for the Indian trade, or material from which these were made; it also quotes G. Dodd (1844): "A kind of cheap cloth, called "stroud" made from woollen rags, was exported to North American Indians." These inventories refer to bolts or pieces of cloth, not blankets.

2 *Capot* "grand pardessus en étoffe ou en fourrure" (Bergeron, 1980, 111). These would have been cloth. The ell (French *aune*) measured 45 inches in England (*OED*) and 1.188 metres or 46¾ inches in France and French Canada (Ledésert and Ledésert, 1972; Bélisle, 1954), and *capots* varying from 4½ *aunes* to 1½ *aunes* appear in inventories. Although the width of these garments is not specified, the largest *capots* would have been very large indeed and, like the Scotsman's plaid, useful when sleeping in the open air.

3 A chief's coat was a sort of uniform given to an influential trading Indian.

4 Molton, "a kind of coarse woollen cloth" (*OED*).

5 Net thread and Holland twine were used in making fishing nets of different meshes. The twine was brought into the country in bulk and tied into net by hand.

6 This object occurs also in other English River Book inventories (pages 118, 122), and in later North West Company inventories, sometimes spelled "maitre de Rétz" (HBCA F.4/1, throughout). *Ritz* or *rétz* is the old-fashioned French word *rets*, a net, which in Canada was pronounced *ré* and meant specifically a gill net (Bélisle, 1954, 1116; *rets* correctly spelled, is used by J.-B. Perrault in his *Relation* [Cormier, 1978, 54]. For the *maître* of a net, probably the stout cord which ran around the outside, to which the net thread was laced, note 44, below.

7 *Moyen*, middle-sized. Small and large sleeves are also mentioned in these inventories.

8 A gun worm was used to clean the residue out of the barrel of a muzzle-loading gun after it had been fired.

9 These awls were probably for making holes in leather to aid in sewing.

10 That is, combs of box-wood.

11 *Milled* here may mean printed calico, although the *OED* notes this only as early as 1839. "Mill'd caps" are frequently mentioned in later inventories.

12 Gartering (*tavelle* in French) seems to have been ribbon or other decorative material used to trim clothing. Later inventories list several varieties, such as *rouge, rayié, jaune, bleu, barré, écossé,* and *fine* (see HBCA F.4/1, 9, 14).

13 Vermilion (red mercuric sulfide) was used extensively by trading Indians for face and body paint.

14 Although the use of *points* on blankets (coloured bars to show their size or value) is now firmly associated with the Hudson's Bay Company, the idea was in use by the Montreal traders by the 1770s, and appears to have been suggested to the Hudson's Bay Company traders by a defecting Canadian, Germain Maugenest (Thorman, 1979).

15 "Cas'd" or "cased," also used in connection with hats eight lines further on and with the same items on page 120, may mean "lined"; *cf*. "cased cats," wildcat skins taken off the animal in such a way that the fur was inside.

16 The Hudson's Bay Company's Athabasca outfit for 1820–1 lists six different kinds of beads, two of which were measured in "bun" (bunches) and the remainder in pounds (Rich, 1983, 142). Other North West Company inventories list many kinds of beads, sometimes counted, but sometimes in masses or bunches (HBCA F.4/3, has examples).

17 "Steels to strike fire from flints" (Rich, 1938, 169 n).

18 Japanned, finished with a black lacquer (*OED*).

19 The same as pillow lace?

20 This item appears again on page 121. It appears to be a phonetic spelling of "none-so-pretties," which is listed in other North West Company inventories, sometimes by the piece, sometimes by the dozen (HBCA F.4/1, 112; F.4/3, 4d). The *OED* lists "none-so-pretty" as a rare, obsolete word, defined as "some article of haberdashery," and gives two instances in the eighteenth century. The exact meaning is apparently unknown.

21 These beads appear again on page 121 as "B. Corn Beads." They were the same as "Beads barley corn," so called probably because of their size, which are listed in the Hudson's Bay Company's Moose Fort standard of trade for 1784 (Rich, 1954, 142), and in other inventories.

22 A skein of worsted yarn.

23 *Couteaux à cartouche*, cartridge knives, used in preparing the charge for a muzzle-loader.

24 Pipes, not necessarily of the ceremonial variety.

25 *Tranche*, a chisel.

26 These tools were assigned to Alexis Derry, evidently to be used in building the new post at Great Slave Lake.

27 Distilled liquor of various kinds.

28 *Agrès*, rigging, tackle. In the Hudson's Bay Company's Athabasca outfit for 1820–1, each canoe had a "cod line, oil cloth, sail & haulyards, sponge, kettle, hatchet, canoe awl, tin pan, gum, bark & wattap" (spruce roots, for sewing bark to the canoe frame), while one canoe in each brigade had a frying pan (Rich, 1938, 166–7).

29 A "piece" was a package of suitable size to be portaged, roughly equal in bulk and weight to a pack of furs. The small items and dry goods on pages 117–18 evidently amounted to six pieces, the "case of irons" was one, and each keg of high wine or powder, each bag of ball or shot, and each bale of tobacco was one piece. The guns and nets were taken as equal to one piece, for a total of 21½ pieces as stated.

30 Aurora, "a rich orange colour, as of the sky at sunrise" (*OED*, noted 1791).

31 See note 15, above.

32 An uncertain reading, which could mean "rum as hogsheads," although the amount of spirits implied is very large, and actual hogsheads (of 52½ imperial gallons) would never had been portaged. In another inventory 120 gallons of *double force* rum was contained in 14 barrels (HBCA F.4/1, 3), for an average content of 8.57 gallons and a weight of almost 86 pounds plus the keg – a typical "piece" of ninety pounds.

33 Japanned boxes containing looking glasses (mirrors) or perhaps drinking tumblers.

34 Tobacco boxes presumably with spring-closed lids.

35 The smallest size of bells in the trade, and the commonest traded. The Hudson's Bay Company's Athabasca outfit for 1820–1 listed 2000 hawks bells, and also 60 dogs bells and 58 horses bells (Rich, 1938, 142–3).

36 This item defeats me. "Nattataned" could just as easily be read "Nallataned" or "Nattalaned," "Coleur" is probably collar.

37 This may have been the North West Company's contribution to religion in the wilderness.

38 Probably *dag* "a kind of heavy pistol or hand-gun formerly in use" (*OED*), though it could also be for *dagger*.

39 See note 21.

40 See note 38.

41 European shoes are more common in fur trade inventories than one would expect. Later inventories list various kinds of shoes, such as "fine Shoes (fine dress)," "common Shoes," "pumps," and "beef shoes," evidently the same as ox hide shoes (see HBCA F.4/1, F.4/3, for examples). Some of these shoes would have been intended for fur traders for full-dress occasions, but the numbers are enough to suggest that some of the working men may have preferred them.

42 Collars.

43 *Casse-tête*, an Indian war-club or tomahawk, but here of European manufacture.

44 The *maîtres* of a net have been defined as ropes used in setting it (Avis, 1967, 457), but the passages quoted there may bear other interpretations. *Maître* can mean an element used to support a construction or maintain its shape; see the sense of canoe gunwale, the first part of the frame to be installed in building a canoe (page 182, note 34). The following passage from J.-B. Perrault's *Relation* seems to explain *maître* of a net: "Il y avoit dans notre reste de marchandise 1ᵗᵇ de fil de couleur

& un maitre de cinq brins, que m^r Bel avoit laissé... Nous tendîmes cette rets le soir..." (Cormier, 1978, 53–54). Here, a makeshift net (*rets*: see note 6 above) was made by tying coloured thread on a *maître* of five strands, and so the *maître* was the stout cord which runs around the outside of the net, and holds the web in shape.

45 *Brayet, brayette* or *bryette* a variant of *braguette,* is said to be used in modern French Canada to mean a bathing costume (Bergeron, 1980, 95, 97) but formerly meant a breechclout.

46 I.e., decorated.

47 From the context, a garment, but unidentified. The reading is uncertain.

48 Except for the portions in sans-serif, this account is entirely in the distinctive handwriting of Joseph Frobisher. Many of the items are quite obscure, but they all involve cash payments. Some are evidently for voyageurs – of the names, Goyette, Picotte, Monette, François and Joseph Fainant, Pagé, Boyer, and Laverdure are all dealt with in appendix B. Frille, Paul, Le Cerfe, Soullier, Allard, Amiott, Adams, La Deboche, Chaurette, Bissonette and L'Ecuyier may all have been voyageurs or clerks working for the Frobishers in different parts of the northwest. For Colonel John Campbell, of the Indian Department in Montreal, who was dabbling in the fur trade at this period, see Leighton (1979), and for Joseph Howard, an old-time fur trader whose best trading days were behind him, see Richardson (1979). Jean-Baptiste Cadotte, a trader at Sault Ste Marie (Armour, 1983b) was supplied by Maurice Blondeau (Béland 1983); Jean-Baptiste Nolin (Chaput, 1987) was probably supplied by Peter Bouthillier of Montreal, and was himself a trader at Michilimackinac and Sault Ste Marie; and Jean-Baptiste Barthe (the elder: see Quaife, 1929, 74 n19, and passim) was also active at Michilimackinac. The money owed these men by the Frobishers was doubtless for provisions or other "country produce" obtained at Michilimackinac or the Sault for the canoe brigades going up to Grand Portage. A point of general significance is that this account shows no debts to be assumed by the North West Company as a whole; rather, the entire English River "adventure," from Montreal all the way to Athabasca, seems to have been conducted as a separate operation. The consolidation of the suppliers at Montreal did not take place until the formation of McTavish, Frobisher & Company in November 1787 (see Wallace, 1934, 75–81).

BIBLIOGRAPHY

MANUSCRIPT SOURCES

Archives nationales du Quebec, Montreal
  CN1–29: Calendar of Notarial Documents from Etude Beek (original)
  Catholic register of Saint-Pierre-de-Sorel (typescript summary copy)

McGill University Libraries and Special Collections, Montreal
  Letter, John Gregory to Simon McTavish, Grand Portage 5 August 1792 (original)
  Journal, summer 1802, kept by F.W. Wentzel at or near Great Slave Lake (photostat)

National Archives of Canada, Ottawa
  MG19, B1–1: North West Company Grand Portage Letter Book (original)
  MG19, C1–4: Lac La Ronge Journal, William McGillivray, 1789–90 (original)
  MG19, C1–5: English River Journal, William McGillivray, (original, undated, but datable to 1793 by internal evidence)
  MG19, C1–15: Peace River Journal, F.W. Wentzel, summer 1800. (I used a partial transcript kindly made available to me by Dr. Mary Black-Rogers.)

Provincial Archives of Manitoba, Winnipeg
  Hudson's Bay Company Archives (originals unless stated)
    A.1/47: Minutes of the London Committee, 1792–9 (microfilm)
    A.5/3: London Letters Outward, General, 1788–96 (microfilm)
    A.32/37: Servants' Contracts
    B.4/a/1: "Pointe au Foutre" post journal, 1795–6
    B.22/a/1 to 5: Brandon House post journals, 1793–8

B.39/a/3, 5ᵃ, 5ᵇ, and 20: "Nottingham House" and Fort Chipewyan post journals, various dates. (Dr Mary Black-Rogers has pointed out to me that the start of the last item is a North West Company journal.)

B.42/a/121a: Churchill Fort post journal, 1794–5

B.49/a/16 to 18: Cumberland House post journals, 1785–7

B.83/a/1: Granville House post journal, 1794–5

B.105/a/1 and 2: Lac La Pluie post journals, 1793–5

B.121/a/1: Manchester House post journal, 1786–7

B.166/a/1 and 2: "Portage de Lisle" post journals, 1793–4

B.199/a/1: "Shell River" post journal, 1794–5

B.205/a/8: South Branch House post journal, 1793–4

B.213/a/1 to 3: Swan River post journals, 1790–3

B.236/a/1: "Winnipeg Lake" post journal, 1796–7

B.239/a/95 and 96: York Factory post journals, 1793–5

B.239/g/1, 2, 4, 6; B.235/g/3: Servants' Accounts, Northern Department, various dates (microfilm)

North West Company Papers (originals)

F.2/1: English River Book, 1786 (printed in full herewith)

F.3/1: Correspondence Inward to Simon McTavish, 1791–9

F.4/1: Ledger for John Sayer & Co, 1795–6 (contains inventories and accounts for trading ventures outfitted by Sayer, as business associate of the North West Company, in the Fond du Lac Department, Lake Superior)

F.4/3: Inventory of North West Company goods remaining in the Montreal warehouse, 1812 (lists over 700 different items, clearly described, with their prices)

F.4/32: Ledger of Servants' Accounts, 1811–21 (microfilm; does not contain accounts for servants in the Columbia, or for *mangeurs du lard*)

F.5/1: Athabasca Servants' Contracts, 1798–1803

F.5/3: Servants' Contracts, 1815–21

Copy No. 626. Diary of Donald Mackay. Photocopy of typed transcript; the manuscript is in private hands. This is a memoir, written no earlier than about 1800, of the writer's adventures in the northwest fur trade and in Canada between 1779 and 1799.

Copy No. 124. "Rocky Mountain Fort" journal, John Thomson, 1800–1. Photostat of original in Masson Collection, McGill University. The post was actually on the Mackenzie River, about two days below the mouth of the Liard.

Selkirk Papers, volume 31. Microfilm copy of handwritten copies in NA. The originals (now lost) were seized by Lord Selkirk from the North West Company in 1816 at Fort William. Apart from miscellaneous records this volume contains a number of fragmentary North West

Company post journals of the first decade of the 1800s, mostly from Athabasca.)

University of Saskatchewan Special Collections, Rare Book Room, University Library
Morton Collection, Fur Trade Licences and Abstracts of Permits. Mss C500/4/2, Volumes 1–3.

PUBLISHED SOURCES

Adney, E.T., and H.I. Chapelle, 1983. *The Bark Canoes and Skin Boats of North America*. Washington: Smithsonian Institution.

APQ Rapport. *Rappport de l'Archiviste de la Province de Québec*. Quebec 1922–3 and other dates.

Armour, D.A. 1983a. "Joseph-Louis Ainsse." *Dictionary of Canadian Biography* 5 (1983): 7–9.

– 1983b. "Jean-Baptiste Cadot". *Dictionary of Canadian Biography* 5 (1983): 128–30.

Avis, W.S., ed. 1967. *A Dictionary of Canadianisms on Historical Principles*. Toronto: W.J. Gage.

Béland, F. 1983. "Maurice-Régis Blondeau." *Dictionary of Canadian Biography* 5 (1983): 89–90.

Bélisle, L.-A. 1954. *Dictionnaire général de la langue française au Canada*. Quebec: Bélisle Éditeur.

Bergeron, L. 1980. *Dictionnaire de la langue québécoise*. Montreal: VLB Éditeur.

Bigsby, J.J. 1969. *The Shoe and Canoe, or Pictures of Travel in the Canadas*. New York: Paladin Press.

Chaput, D. 1987. "Jean-Baptiste Nolin." *Dictionary of Canadian Biography* 6 (1987): 546–8.

Charbonneau, H., and J. Légaré, eds. 1980–8. *Répertoire des actes de baptême, mariage, sépulture, et des recensements du Québec ancien*. Montreal: Les Presses de l'Université de Montréal.

Cormier, Louis-P., ed. 1978. *Jean-Baptiste Perrault, marchand voyageur, parti de Montréal le 28ᵉ de mai 1783*. Montreal: Boréal Express.

Coues, E., ed. 1965. *New Light on the Early History of the Greater Northwest*. Minneapolis: Ross and Haines.

Davidson, G.C. 1967. *The North West Company*. New York: Russell and Russell.

Douglas, R., ed. 1929. *Nipigon to Winnipeg: A Canoe Voyage through Western Ontario by Edward Umfreville in 1784, with Extracts from the Writings of Other Early Travellers Through the Region*. Ottawa: Commercial Printing.

Epp, Henry T., and Tim Jones, 1969. "The Methy Portage – Proposal for a Saskatchewan Historic and Nature Trail." *The Blue Jay*, 27 (1969): 101–7.

Faribault-Beauregard, M. 1982. *La population des forts français d'Amérique (XVIIIᵉ siècle)*, Vol. 1. Montreal: Éditions Bergeron.

Gates, C.M., ed. 1965. *Five Fur Traders of the North West*. 2nd ed. St Paul: Minnesota Historical Society.

Gough, B.M. 1983. "Peter Pond." *Dictionary of Canadian Biography* 5 (1983): 681–6.

Harmon, D.W. 1973. *A Journal of Voyages and Travels in the Interior of North America*. New York: AMS Press.

Henry, A. 1969. *Travels and Adventures in Canada and the Indian Territories between the Years 1760 and 1776*. Rutland and Tokyo, Charles E. Tuttle Co.

Innis, H.A. 1927. "The North West Company." *Canadian Historical Review* 8: 308–21.

– 1930. *Peter Pond, Fur Trader and Adventurer*. Toronto: Irwin and Gordon.

– 1970. *The Fur Trade in Canada*. Toronto: University of Toronto Press.

International Genealogical Index. 1988 ed. Microfiche publication of the Genealogical Society of the Church of Jesus Christ of Latter Day Saints: Salt Lake City.

Jenness, D. 1977. *The Indians of Canada*. 7th ed. Toronto: University of Toronto Press.

Jetté, R. 1983. *Dictionnaire généalogique des familles du Québec*. Montreal: Les Presses de l'Université de Montréal.

Johnson, A.M., ed. 1967. *Saskatchewan Journals and Correspondence*. London: Hudson's Bay Record Society Publication no 26.

Lamb, W. Kaye, ed. 1960. *The Journals and Letters of Simon Fraser 1806–1808*. Toronto: Macmillan.

– 1970. *The Journals and Letters of Sir Alexander Mackenzie*. Toronto: Macmillan.

Lareau, P.J., and F.J. Hamelin, eds. 1984. *Manitoba Marriages/Mariages du Manitoba*. Ottawa: Le Centre de Généalogie S.C.

Ledésert, R.P.L, and M. Ledésert. 1972. *Harrap's New Standard French and English Dictionary*, Revised ed. London: Harrap.

Leighton, D. 1979. "John Campbell." *Dictionary of Canadian Biography* 4 (1979): 129–31.

Long, J. 1791. *Voyages and Travels of an Indian Interpreter and Trader*. London: for the author.

MacGregor, J.G. 1966. *Peter Fidler, Canada's Forgotten Surveyor*. Toronto: McClelland and Stewart.

Mackenzie, A. 1801. *Voyages from Montreal on the River St. Laurence through the Continent of North America to the Frozen and Pacific Oceans*. London: T. Cadell.

McLeod, M. 1971. *Peace River. A Canoe Voyage from Hudson's Bay to Pacific.* Rutland and Tokyo: Charles E. Tuttle Co.

MacLeod, M.A., and W.L. Morton. 1974. *Cuthbert Grant of Grantown*, 2nd ed. Toronto: McClelland and Stewart.

Masson, L.R., ed. 1960. *Les Bourgeois de la Compagnie du Nord-Ouest.* New York: Antiquarian Press.

Merk, F., ed. 1968. *Fur Trade and Empire. George Simpson's Journal 1824–5.* 2nd ed. Cambridge, Mass.: Belknap Press of Harvard University.

Morice, A.G. 1905. *History of the Northern Interior of British Columbia.* 3rd ed. Toronto: William Briggs.

Morton, A.S., ed. 1929. *The Journal of Duncan McGillivray.* Toronto: Macmillan.

– 1937. "Forrest Oakes, Charles Boyer, Joseph Fulton and Peter Pangman in the North-West, 1765–1793." Royal Society of Canada, *Transactions*, Section II, 1937: 87–100.

– 1973. *A History of the Canadian West to 1870–71.* 2nd ed., edited by L.G. Thomas. Toronto and Buffalo: University of Toronto Press.

PAC *Report*, 1939. Public Archives of Canada, Ottawa.

Parker, J.M. 1976. "The Struggle for the Athabasca." In L.H. Thomas, ed., *Essays on Western History.* Edmonton: University of Alberta Press.

Payment, D.P. 1987. "Jean-Baptiste Letendre, *dit* Batoche." *Dictionary of Canadian Biography* 6 (1987): 398–9.

Quaife, M.M., ed. 1928. *The John Askin Papers.* Vol. 1. Detroit: Detroit Library Commission.

Rich, E.E., ed. 1938. *Journal of Occurences in the Athabasca Department by George Simpson, 1820 and 1821.* London: Hudson's Bay Record Society Publication no 1.

– 1941. *The Letters of John McLoughlin from Fort Vancouver to the Governor and Committee. First Series, 1825–28.* London: Hudson's Bay Record Society Publication no 4.

– 1949. *James Isham's Observations on Hudsons Bay, 1743, and Notes and Observations on a book entitled A Voyage to Hudsons Bay in the Dobbs Galley, 1749.* London: Hudson's Bay Record Society Publication no 12.

– 1951. *Cumberland House Journals and Inland Journal, 1775–82. First Series, 1775–79.* London: Hudson's Bay Record Society Publication no 14.

– 1952. *Cumberland House Journals and Inland Journal, 1775–82. Second Series, 1780–82.* London: Hudson's Bay Record Society Publication no 15.

– 1954. *Moose Fort Journals, 1783–85.* London: Hudson's Bay Record Society Publication no 17.

– 1955. *A Journal of a Voyage from Rocky Mountain Portage in Peace River to the Sources of Finlays Branch and North West Ward in Summer 1824.* London: Hudson's Bay Record Society Publication no 18.

– 1959. *The History of the Hudson's Bay Company, 1670–1870*. Vol. II. London: Hudson's Bay Record Society Publication no 22.

Richardson, A.J.H. 1979. "Joseph Howard." *Dictionary of Canadian Biography* 4 (1979): 369–70.

Sloan, W.A. 1987. "Aw-gee-nah (English Chief)." *Dictionary of Canadian Biography* 6 (1987): 20.

Sprague, D.N., and R.P. Frye. 1983. *The Genealogy of the First Metis Nation*. Winnipeg: Pemmican Publications.

Tanguay, C. 1871–90. *Dictionnaire généalogique des familles canadiennes*. Quebec: Eusèbe Senécal.

Thorman, G.E. 1979. "Germain Maugenest." *Dictionary of Canadian Biography* 4 (1979): 524–5.

Tyrrell, J.B., ed. 1968a. *Journals of Samuel Hearne and Philip Turnor*. New York: Greenwood Press.

– 1968b. *David Thompson's Narrative of his Explorations in Western America, 1784–1812*. New York: Greenwood Press.

Wagner, H.A. 1955. *Peter Pond, Fur Trader and Explorer*. New Haven: Yale University Press.

Wallace, J.N. 1929. *The Wintering Partners on Peace River from the Earliest Records to the Union in 1821*. Ottawa: Thorburn and Abbott.

Wallace, W.S., ed. 1934. *Documents Relating to the North West Company*. Toronto: Champlain Society.

– 1954. *The Pedlars from Quebec and Other Papers on the Nor'Westers*. Toronto: Ryerson Press.

Williams, G., ed. 1969. *Andrew Graham's Observations on Hudson's Bay, 1767–91*. London: Hudson's Bay Record Society Publication no 27.

– 1973. *London Correspondence Inward from Sir George Simpson, 1841–42*. London: Hudson's Bay Record Society Publication no 31.

INDEX